We welcome this work with its leve
the body of knowledge! It is a con
sion, the church, the Lamba people, ...y ...
dawned that has ushered in a new era of non-western contribution to the
history of Christian mission. While this work by Conrad Mbewe is a maiden
academic work, it is nonetheless a monumental contribution to Christian
history. Writing from the margins, yet enriching the majority. The writing
of this thesis is the raising of a voice once not heard. Subjects of indigenization, contextualization, theologizing, initiation of church and leadership
are methodically articulated and presented with in-depth original research.
Africa and the world stand to benefit from this positively depicted experience
despite it being steeped in the realities of colonial and ecclesiastical historical inequalities.

Dr Lazarus Phiri
Principal of the Theological College of Central Africa, Zambia

During my pilgrimage as pastor, church planter, and seminary professor I
have read numerous articles, books, master and doctoral theses, on practically all facets of missiology. But I have always observed a gap in missiological
literature regarding the contribution of 'nationals' from the majority world,
especially from the global south, in the areas of principles of successful biblical church planting. Therefore, I am first of all thankful to the Lord for Dr
Conrad Mbewe's research on the faithful, fruitful, fearless living, work, and
teaching of Paul Kasonga and Olive Doke in Zambia. Second, I am also
thankful that Conrad offered a biblical and theological foundation in order to
understand and put in perspective the great contribution and lessons found
throughout their ministry. And third, Conrad was able to present in detail
a church planting model whose principles are biblically grounded and ap-
plicable anywhere. More works such as this one ought to be read and spread.

Rev Elias Medeiros, PhD
Harriet Barbour Professor of Mission and Missions Department Chairman
Reformed Theological Seminary
Jackson, MS, USA

As one who has had the task of reading through many postgraduate theses I can say that very rarely does one find genuinely scholarly work combined with deep spiritual insight and sheer reading enjoyment! Such is the case with Conrad Mbewe's landmark study on the lives of Olive Doke and Paul Kasonga and the insights provided for mission and church planting today. The book is filled with fascinating biographical details and most important insights on the great work of handing on the gospel and handing over the work of the gospel to those who have received it. This work has value far beyond Africa, indeed, for the whole world and to everyone who has caught the vision of spreading the good news to the ends of the earth and establishing communities of Christ's followers in every nation and people.

Dr Kevin Roy
Church Historian and Pastor
Muldersdrift Union Church, South Africa

Insights from the Lives of Olive Doke and Paul Kasonga for Pioneer Mission and Church Planting Today

Conrad Mbewe

MONOGRAPHS

© 2014 by Conrad Mbewe

Published 2014 by Langham Monographs
an imprint of Langham Creative Projects

Langham Partnership
PO Box 296, Carlisle, Cumbria CA3 9WZ, UK
www.langham.org

ISBNs:
978-1-78368-924-8 Print
978-1-78368-922-4 Mobi
978-1-78368-923-1 ePub
978-1-78368-889-0 PDF

British Library Cataloguing in Publication Data

Mbewe, Conrad, author.
  Insights from the lives of Olive Doke and Paul Kasonga for
  pioneer mission and church planting today.
  1. Church development, New. 2. Evangelistic work. 3. Church
  development, New--Baptists. 4. Church development, New--
  Zambia--Kafulafuta--History--20th century. 5. Doke,
  Olive. 6. Kassonga, Paul.
  I. Title
  254.1-dc23

  ISBN-13: 9781783689248

Cover & Book Design: projectluz.com

Contents

Preface and Acknowledgments

The research involved in the writing of this book has been most rewarding. I began this research because during my MA studies, I stumbled across a very rare gem – the relationship between Olive Doke and Paul Kasonga. I could not help thinking that there was something in that relationship that we could all learn from, especially as we engage in the work of missions. I was aware, from my little experience in church planting missions, that the handover process from missionaries to indigenous leaders has often been a very rough part of the Great Commission ride. Complaints have often come from both sides. What was it that made things so different between Olive Doke and Paul Kasonga? It was this curiosity that got the better of me and started me off on this research. As I have already stated, what I found was most rewarding. It is my prayer that many missionaries and indigenous leaders will use the fruit of this research to correct the attitudes that often feed into wrong handover processes in missions.

This has been a labour of love. However, to bring it to completion, I have benefitted from the help of many people. The list below is not exhaustive. However, I hope I will not fail to include those whose help stands out head-and-shoulders above the others.

- The first person I would like to thank is my wife, Felistas, without whose encouragement I would not have reached this far in my studies. She never begrudged me the many hours that I left her alone because I needed to push this research further. Even when I needed to use household funds to pay for research assistance, she gave me the much-needed nod to press on. Thank you, my dear.
- Then I must remember my children – Bwalya, Mwila, Mwindula, Mwansa, and Mwape. Your love for the work of

Christ in his church on earth encouraged me to soldier on, knowing that this was one investment you would also be interested in. I can only hope that my example will challenge you to go as far as you can go in your educational pursuits also – for the glory of God.

- Then I must thank the church officers and members of Kabwata Baptist Church for two things. The first is your love for the work of missions, which has caused you to send out missionaries across Zambia and even beyond. It was because of this that I saw the need to "do it right" where so many others have been doing it wrong. The second reason why I must thank you is that you have willingly financed a large portion of the cost of these studies and have been willing to allow me time off to ensure that the job is done. This is your achievement.

- Yet another "thank you" goes to my two official church assistants. Seke Lupunga (my ministry assistant), you took on this project as if it was your own. If a degree could be shared between two people, I could have given you the other half. Patience Namangala Mukubuta (my office assistant), you picked up anything that fell off Seke's table and gladly put it onto your plate, despite the fact that your own plate was always full. Thank you for showing me what it means to joyfully serve God.

- The librarians and archivists at the Baptist Theological College in Johannesburg (South Africa) and at the Baptist Theological Seminary in Lusaka (Zambia) were very helpful in allowing me the use of their libraries and resources. Without your help, this would have been like fixing a car without tools – an impossible task.

- Then how can I forget Amon and Ivon Silwimba, who allowed me the use of their Dream Valley Lodge whenever I needed to hide away from people for days to concentrate on the PhD research? The lovely serene surroundings of the lodge had a cooling effect on the CPU between my two ears as it worked in overdrive.

- Finally, I must thank two individuals who have brought me to the end of this journey. These are Professor Nelus Niemandt, the Head of the Department of the Science of Religion and Missiology at the University of Pretoria, and Dr Lindsay Rinquest, the Principal of the Cape Town Baptist Seminary. The former was my supervisor and the latter was my co-supervisor for this thesis. How you managed to give me the time and counsel in the midst of your very demanding jobs, I do not know. All I can say is that I hope I can emulate your humility and servant hearts.

Abstract

In this book, the researcher observes that one of the most difficult phases in the work of church-planting missions is that of the handover stage from pioneer missionaries to indigenous leaders. This is often fraught with suspicion and fighting, and hence tends to delay the work until such issues are finally dealt with. Having observed a different story in the relationship between Olive Doke and Paul Kasonga in the early years of establishing the Baptist work in Zambia, the researcher has argued that the key lay in their mutual respect and admiration. He therefore posits that where these two ingredients are nurtured in the early stages of missions there will be a smooth handover process.

In order to show that this was not just a philosophical or pragmatic idea, the researcher began his work with a biblical interpretation of missions. Drawing from the way the Lord Jesus Christ and his apostles went about their own handing over process to the next generation of leaders, he identified these same attitudes of mutual respect and admiration. He argues that these played an important role in ensuring a meaningful handover process.

The researcher then entered upon finding as much information as he could on the lives of Olive Doke and Paul Kasonga, and about their working relationship. This was through unearthing various archived materials and conducting key interviews in the region where they once laboured. This formed the core of this research and, upon subjecting this to analysis, it proved the theory that the success of their working relationship and handover process at the Kafulafuta Mission lay in their mutual respect and admiration.

Finally, the researcher offers a model or strategy to ensure that what may have happened inadvertently between Olive Doke and Paul Kasonga is nurtured among missionaries and indigenous leaders. The researcher works these principles into all the stages of church planting missions – all the way from the training of the missionaries to the time when the work is totally handed over into the hands of local leaders and the missionaries have withdrawn from the work.

CHAPTER 1

Focus of this Research

1.1 Introduction

This research is about the handover process in pioneer church-planting missions, which must inevitably take place as the terminus of missions work. Church-planting missions work must end with self-governing, self-supporting and self-propagating churches, as Henry Venn and Ruff Anderson asserted (Little 2005). This research, therefore, deals with the question of how best to engage in the process of pioneering missionaries handing over their work to indigenous leaders so that the process becomes a blessing rather than a curse – as it has often proved to be. It looks at the example of two individuals, Olive Doke and Paul Kasonga, who exemplified how this handover process is to be done in a sensitive and mature manner. There is much that the church today can learn from these two individuals. This researcher's thesis, proved by what he sees in these two individuals, is that a sensitive handover process is not built on mere systems and agreements, but on a foundation of mutual respect and growing admiration between pioneer missionaries and indigenous leaders.

In a broader sense, therefore, this research is relevant to the (African) church's unfinished task of missions, especially to its rural areas and also to those regions that still lie largely unevangelized, what the experts in missions call the 10/40 window. Many of these areas still need pioneer missions work, resulting in the planting of viable and strong churches. The church in Africa, and more specifically in Zambia, needs to rise to this challenge. This researcher hopes that his research will play a small role in rousing the church in Zambia to put aside its many excuses in order to put its shoulders to the wheel of missions today, especially in areas still needing pioneer work. Meiring expresses this hope when he says:

> Many problems beset the African Church from within as well as from without. Africa is still a continent filled with bloodshed and violence, a hungry and poor continent, where illiteracy, uncontrolled urbanization, lack of planning, housing, and sanitation create seemingly insoluble problems. Political strife is tearing Africa apart . . . Racism and tribalism abound. Islam and Marxism deny the church its message. But the church is a factor in the new Africa! The river of witness flows wide and deep and swiftly. More than 6 million Africans are added to the church every year, at an astonishing rate of 16,608 believers a day. Perhaps the day will break . . . when Africa will seize its opportunity to proclaim the gospel in the world, to open doors to India and China and Japan, hitherto closed to white Christians. 'If the African church could accept this challenge, Africa not only would numerically grow into the largest Christian continent, but become the most important torch bearer of the gospel of Christ upon the earth.' (Meiring 1980, 24).

The researcher also hopes that his research will help the church in Zambia avoid one of the major mistakes that has been repeated over and over again in missions, and which has been a bottleneck in the progress of missions; namely, the bad relationships between pioneering missionaries and local Christian leaders. Mulemfo refers to the mistakes that western missionaries made and also warns Africans of repeating these mistakes if they do not learn from them. He writes:

> It is true that missionaries made many mistakes, some deliberate and others out of their ignorance of the people and their contextual realities. A possible explanation is that the missionaries did not equate themselves as human beings on

the same level as the missionized. . . . Africans should begin to understand that if they can make mistakes, then missionaries could also make mistakes in their missionary work in Africa. In a similar set of circumstances, there is no guarantee that Africans would not also commit mistakes in their missionary endeavour (Mulemfo 2001, 11).

Huneycutt refers to this when she writes:

> The Third Era has revealed that there are still many people groups where the church does not exist, and they require a pioneering strategy. However, today the pioneering is being accomplished by Western and non-Western mission structures. What is necessary now is partnership in pioneering. The non-Western church is in many ways on an equal footing with the Western church in finishing the remaining task. Because the people groups remaining to be reached are non-Western themselves, the Western church has much it can learn from its Majority World partners. Likewise, the non-Western church has much it can learn from the mistakes and successes of 200 years of Protestant mission (Honeycutt 2009, 381).

What Huneycutt is saying here, is that there have been mistakes and successes in missions work in the past. As we partner together to finish the remaining task of missions, we need to learn from the past so that we do not repeat the mistakes that were committed then, and also so that we emulate the good examples that were there in the past. One of the areas where these mistakes have been made has been in the handover process from missionaries to indigenous leaders. Hence the available successful examples, such as the case between Olive Doke and Paul Kasonga, should be known, studied and emulated.

1.1.1 Why the subject of missions is still relevant today

Why should we bother with missions to the point of wanting to urge this generation of Christians to risk their lives for it? It is because the work of missions is at the very centre of history. This is the chief work that God is doing. He is extending the borders of his kingdom. Jesus taught us to pray, "Our Father, who is in heaven, hallowed be your name. Your kingdom come. Your will be done, on earth as it is in heaven." (Matt 6:9–10). If that is not about missions, then this researcher does not know what is! David Bosch, in his magnum opus, *Transforming Mission*, says:

> The Christian faith, I submit, is intrinsically missionary. . . .
> The Christian faith, for example, sees "all generations of the earth" as objects of God's salvific will and plan of salvation or, in New Testament terms, it regards the 'reign of God' which has come in Jesus Christ as intended for 'all humanity' (cf. Oecumenische Inleiding 1988, 19). This dimension of the Christian faith is not an optional extra: Christianity is missionary by its very nature, or it denies its very *raison d'être* (Bosch 1991, 11).

In fact, it can be argued that the whole Bible is about missions. Christopher J. H. Wright, in his book, *The Mission of God*, makes the sweeping statement, "Mission is, in my view, a major key that unlocks the whole grand narrative of the canon of Scripture" (2006, 17). In other words, missions is the metanarrative of the whole Bible. So, even before we look at the historical study that makes up the research, the researcher intends to look at a few major passages in Scripture that not only show the importance of this study but also give some examples of how pioneer missions work was undertaken under the leadership of Christ and his apostles. Coming from an evangelical tradition, it is important that the researcher establishes what he is saying from Scripture. Only after that will we come to the case study in Zambia and appreciate the history we will be examining and the challenge that lies before the church in this nation.

1.1.2 The nation and region in which this study is based

Zambia is the country in which our case study is based. It lies in the southern half of Africa, and it is right in the centre of that southern half. It is landlocked, and surrounded by eight countries – Angola, Namibia, Botswana,

Zimbabwe, Mozambique, Malawi, Tanzania, and the Democratic Republic of Congo. It became a sovereign state in 1964, having previously been under British colonial rule. During its colonial days it was known as Northern Rhodesia (while present day Zimbabwe was known as Southern Rhodesia), and almost all the history that we shall be looking at will be during those colonial days.

The specific region in Zambia where our case study in this work is based is now called the Copperbelt Province. At that time it was called Lambaland, because it was an area largely inhabited by the Lamba-speaking people. Although today this region is perhaps the most densely populated and developed in the whole of Zambia, at the start of the story being researched and used as the basis of this work – prior to the discovery of copper – it was the least developed, with hardly any white people there. Many church missionary bodies were already operating in many other parts of Northern Rhodesia when the Baptists began their work in the country and they found that the Lambas were still with no Christian witness among them. They were, as it were, 'the last frontier' in this country.

An appreciation of the place that the Copperbelt Province began to occupy in the economy of the country during the period under study helps to explain some of the challenges that had to be faced by the pioneers whose lives are at the centre of this research. Munkumba, in his research on the copper mines in Zambia, writes:

> According to Fraser and Lungu (2007), one of the world's largest sources of copper ore is found on the border of Zambia and the DRC in a region known as the Copperbelt. The first commercial mine was opened in 1928 and mining has dominated Zambia's economy since then. In 1969, Zambia was classified a middle-income country, with one of the highest GDPs in Africa, three times that of Kenya, twice that of Egypt, and higher than Brazil, Malaysia, Turkey and South Korea (18). By 1973, Zambia had an urban population of 1 million out of a total population of 4 million. 750,000 were in waged employment. In 1968, Zambia nationalized the

mines and formed the Zambia Consolidated Copper Mines
(ZCCM). (Munkumba 2008, 7).

All these historic changes took place during the period under study and
largely in the same area being researched on.

1.1.3 The church denomination in which this study is based

This researcher's reason for going to the history of the Baptist denomination in Zambia to find two heroes of the faith is that very little research
has been done on this, and yet it is certainly one successful story of pioneer missions and church planting on the African continent. The absence
of well-researched information came to the researcher's attention when
Baptists in Zambia were celebrating their one-hundredth anniversary
(1905–2005). The researcher looked in vain for a book that captured this
history. Fragments of this history were available in a few theses and books
in the libraries of theological colleges and also in the Zambian national
archives. But no comprehensive history was available anywhere. Hence, he
decided to do the research himself and come up with some comprehensive
account. The fruit of this research makes up much of the thesis for his
Master of Arts degree (Mbewe 2007). It was not long into this research
before he realised that he had stumbled across some heroic figures and feats
that were well worth documenting and publicising. He also realised that
the *modus operandi* of these heroes of the faith was well worth emulating
today (Mbewe 2007, 74).

One conviction the researcher got as a result of his Master of Arts research was that the success in planting the Baptist denomination in Zambia
was not accidental. It was because of the dedication *and deliberate strategy*
of those who laboured during the pioneer stage of the work. There were
many forces against them, which would have made men and women of
lesser dedication give up the work long before. Finances to keep the missionaries in the field were always a problem, and so many of them had to
raise their own finances to remain in the field. The mission field was infest-
ed with malaria-carrying mosquitoes, ferocious wild animals, and poison-
ous snakes. Many missionaries either died or returned home early because

of this. Also, in the midst of all this was the need to learn the language of the indigenous people, reduce it into written communication, teach the indigenous people how to read and write, translate the Bible and other relevant books into the language of the indigenous people, etc. While all this was going on, the work of evangelism and discipleship was at the heart of everything. Converts were slow to come in, but the labourers persevered. In due season local leadership began to emerge.

In this work, the researcher wants to show that care was taken in the handing over process so that the churches that were planted were given into the hands of properly qualified men – the first indigenous leaders of the Baptist church in Zambia. It is partly because of the carefulness in the handing-over process that a strong foundation for the Baptist church in Zambia was laid. By looking at the life of one missionary and one early indigenous church leader, we shall have a window through which we can observe this careful handing-over process.

1.1.4 The interest of this researcher in this research

The baton is now in our hands. Those who laboured in the pioneering days have all gone to their rest. There is a lot we can learn from those stalwarts of the faith as we also venture into new spheres where the gospel has not yet taken root. Hence, the researcher's interest is not purely historical but also pastoral. He does not just want to document what happened in those early years of the Baptist denominational history in Zambia; he wants us to learn afresh how to do pioneer missions and church planting from this segment of church history. Therefore, this is a historical-missiological study. It looks back into church history to learn from those who have gone before us and also looks forward to the challenge of missions that still awaits the church, especially the Zambian church, in its quest to fulfil the Great Commission that Jesus left us with. The lessons learned from history will inform us about how best to fulfil the challenge of pioneer missions work today.

1.1.4.1 Personal motivation

The researcher is a church pastor. The church that he has been pastoring for the last twenty-five years – the Kabwata Baptist Church – is currently in the process of planting churches in no less than twenty places (i.e. cities, towns, suburbs, and villages) in Zambia and in neighbouring countries. More doors are still opening up. He is concerned that his church's missionaries do not end up falling in the same ditch that other pioneer missionaries have fallen into when they come to the terminal stage of handing over the work to indigenous leaders. This is what has particularly interested him in this study. As Mouton warns:

> Although one's motivation is usually a combination of intrinsic and external rewards, most people, including your supervisor, would advise you not to pursue a master's or doctoral project solely because of the anticipated extrinsic rewards. If your only or primary reason for enrolling in a postgraduate programme is because you wish to enhance your career prospects, you are doing so for the wrong reasons. This is even more relevant for doctoral studies than for master's studies . . . If you have no interest whatsoever in the pursuit of knowledge, but are doing the master's or doctoral studies purely for professional or other extrinsic reasons, you must definitely reconsider your decision! (2001, 5)

Once we take the work of pioneer missions seriously, we will soon face the same struggles that others before us faced. One of them will be the tact necessary to ensure that the terminus point in missions – the handing over of the work to indigenous leaders – is done well. This will not happen automatically. One of the challenges in pioneer missions work is the lack of converts to write home about, who must ultimately become the leaders into whose hands we must hand over the work. Learning from the past will keep us going despite such apparent barrenness. "Learning to be patient in pioneer situations" is one of the lessons to be learned from a documented history of the church (Mbewe 2007, 74–75).

1.1.4.2 Denominational motivation
It is fairly evident from the reading of Baptist work in Zambia that this problem has surfaced a number of times. One typical example is what transpired between the Baptist Mission of Zambia (the pioneer missionaries) and

the Baptist Convention of Zambia (the indigenous leadership). Thomas Kasongo Lumba documents this very well in *A Quest for Authentic Practice of Missions in Africa* (1995).

Whatever may be said in the course of finger pointing, it must be admitted that even in this late stage of Baptist life in Zambia, there was lack of sensitivity in the shared leadership of the churches between the Baptist Convention of Zambia and the Baptist Mission of Zambia. The partnership was vulnerable due to a lack of trust and mutual respect. And, although this finally found expression in the split of an entire Baptist denomination, it must have started at a personal level where individual church leaders failed to work together in a state of mutual respect. Put more positively, what guarantees harmony at an institutional level is harmony at a personal level. And this will only take place where there is mutual respect. The example of Olive Doke and Paul Kasonga should challenge all of us to improve in this area.

1.1.4.3 Contemporary motivation

Yet this was not a problem that remained in the wider denomination's history. It is one that the researcher has met with again and again, including during the research period. Pioneer missionaries complain about the behaviour of indigenous leaders that make it difficult for them to be entrusted with the keys of the mission. Indigenous leaders also complain about the lack of transparency of missionaries that makes it difficult for them to trust them.

During the interviews related to this research, Curtis Chirwa, an indigenous leader wrote:

> The reasons for this [frustration], is because of the unfulfilled promises missionaries tend to give to nationals whom they know will never be in charge completely. Hence, making a national pastor to work with false hopes, which later bring frustrations in life and work. Many missionaries live lives that are not compatible with the lessons they teach the nationals. I worked with four different missionaries, which

would be enough experience for me to make an assessment (Chirwa 2010).

Surely, this lack of mutual trust and respect cannot auger well for the future of missions. Thus, the researcher has been burdened to find a solution to it. Again, his eyes were directed to Olive Doke and Paul Kasonga to see what the secret was of their seamless working relationship and handover process.

It became evident to this researcher that having done a bird's-eye-view of the Baptist work in Zambia over its first one hundred years in his Master of Arts thesis, it was important for the researcher to now zero-in on the two individuals who played a decisive role in this history. Such a biographical study would be meaningful. This is because the great strides made by the church in its history are primarily because of a few individuals who were gripped by the grandeur of the work of the gospel and, therefore, gave their lives for the extension of God's kingdom. We miss a lot if we remain in a position where all we are seeing is the macro-picture, without coming down close enough to the situation in order to see the micro-picture. We must not allow the breath-taking panoramic view of the forest to make us fail to see the beauty of the individual trees that make up that forest.

1.1.5 The individuals chosen for the case study

In order to zero-in on a few individuals, as already stated, the researcher has chosen Olive Doke and Paul Kasonga quite deliberately as the individuals to research and learn from. They were not the ones who first began the work of Baptists in Zambia. In that sense, he ought to have done research on Henry Masters and Arthur Philips, who started Kafulafuta mission in 1905. So, why has he skipped these two men and instead chosen Olive Doke and Paul Kasonga?

1.1.5.1 The choice of Olive Doke

The researcher has chosen Olive Doke for a number of reasons. She went to Lambaland in 1916 and laboured there until she died in 1972 – fifty-six years later! She is, arguably, the longest-serving Baptist missionary in the history of Zambia. Therefore, her biography is like a string on which we can hang most of the story of the first sixty-six years of Baptist history in

Zambia. Anyone who wants to understand how God worked in the pioneer stage of Baptist history in Zambia need only look at the life of this one woman. This researcher has also chosen her because she was a woman and was single all her life. Olive left the comforts of the city of Johannesburg in South Africa at the age of twenty-five and went to Lambaland when it was virtually all bush. She was not following a husband, as was the case with many female missionaries in those days. She went on her own. Talk about the kind of sacrifice required in pioneer missions work and you have it tied up in this one woman! This researcher has also chosen her because there is still no biography written and published on Olive Doke despite her great accomplishment in Lambaland. He has to work from fragments in unpublished works, theses, reports, and magazines in archives. There is need to change this. This heroine deserves a biography that can be put side by side with those of David Livingstone and William Carey.

Olive Doke participated in the translation of the first Lamba Bible and wrote many readers, primers and other educational and religious materials in Lamba. She helped to translate many of the old English hymns into Lamba. It is difficult to think of a role that this remarkable woman did not play. Someone has said that Olive was "a bricklayer, carpenter, printer, Bible teacher, nurse, translator, hunter, teacher, gardener, evangelist, preacher, pastor, church organiser and whatever else was needed on the field" (Kretzschmar 1996, 1). Another church historian has written, "With the arrival of Olive Doke at KMS, a chapter in missionary history had begun which, it could be argued, was to be one of the most influential of any one missionary anywhere. Olive was to spend the rest of her life amongst the Lambas and the record of her activities and influence is simply outstanding" (Kemp 1987, 66). Surely, this woman deserves to be better known than she is today!

1.1.5.2 The choice of Paul Kasonga

The researcher has also chosen Paul Kasonga because he was the very first local leader of the Baptist church in Zambia. In terms of conversion, he was preceded by quite a number of other indigenous people, the most prominent one having been Chief Katanga's son, Sandabunga, who was converted in 1908 (Frey 2009, 39) and baptized in 1910. Sandabunga even became an evangelist, preaching the gospel to his fellow indigenous people, before Kasonga was even converted! However, in terms of official recognition as a leader of the Baptist church – with actual church authority – Paul Kasonga was the first. In other words, he was the first local person to whom the missionaries first gave actual leadership and authority. This was a very significant step in the development of the church in Zambia and it seems to have taken place in 1931, because that was when Paul Kasonga's name first appeared as one of the leaders of the mission on the cover of *Lambaland*, the official newsletter of the Baptist missionaries labouring in that area. For the next three years, his was the only name (together with that of A. J. Cross and O. C. Doke) until Anasi Lupunga joined him in 1934. Lupunga was to assist Kasonga as he pastored the Kafulafuta mission church until he (Kasonga) died twenty years later.

Very little is written about Kasonga relative to the many fragments on Olive Doke. This was because, as Natasha Erlank rightly observes, "Our knowledge of African agency is circumscribed, however, by the missionary preference for describing their own work in the surviving records" (Erlank 2003, 31). However, anyone who reads the little that has been written about him soon discovers why this man became the acknowledged leader of the work among the indigenous people. This researcher has also chosen him because he was a leper, and in fact, died at a relatively young age of about fifty because of complications arising from this illness. The fact that the early missionaries chose a leper to be the first official local leader of the church is in itself worth stating, studying, and possibly even commending. Like God, whom they sought to serve, they looked at the inward person and not at the outward man, which was being eaten away by that dreaded disease. In Paul Kasonga we have an example of a person who suffered much and whose testimony shone even brighter because of his suffering.

In his doctoral thesis, based on the Baptist churches in South Africa, Timothy Cantrell says that,

> the central theoretical argument of this study is that, despite the rapid numerical growth in church planting in the BUSA and across Africa, many churches are not maturing because they have not been properly evangelized and established.

Leadership has not been effectively entrusted to qualified local elders, with sad results. It is expected that the research will
reveal that many recent BUSA churches (especially those in
the Baptist Northern Association, near where the researcher
lives and ministers) are in grave danger of nominalism if they
are not strengthened in such areas as qualified eldership, interpretation and applying Scripture, discipling and equipping
members, and effective church planting. These weaknesses
will be corrected only by a commitment to biblical strategies
for planting and building churches toward maturity (Cantrell
2004, 7).

In Paul Kasonga, and others of his spiritual stature, the danger mentioned
by Cantrell was prevented as the church in Lambaland was being established. This needs to be seen and appreciated as today's church considers
new spheres for church planting.

1.1.5.3 Why two individuals

Normally, in a work like this, one would expect that only one case study
would be used. Why then has this researcher chosen to use two individuals? It is because the burden of his thesis is to show from this case study
how missionaries and indigenous people *should work together* in harmony,
mutual respect, and admiration, if the work of pioneer missions will give
birth to healthy church planting. A 'handover' process is key at some stage
to the establishment of the work. We see this in the relationship between
these two individuals. Olive Doke and Paul Kasonga had a real brotherly
affection, deep respect, and unfeigned admiration for each other. This was
despite the many differences between them: Doke was white, but Kasonga
was black. Olive was female, while Kasonga was male. Doke was a missionary, but Kasonga was a local person. Doke grew up in the comforts of the
developed world, while Kasonga grew up in a rural village. Doke enjoyed
very good health, but Kasonga was a sickly leper. One would expect a lot
of problems between the two because of all these differences and yet they
bonded together very well.

There are a few documents written (or, perhaps, dictated) by Paul Kasonga that are extant today that show how much respect and admiration he had for Olive Doke. Long before the South African Baptist Missionary Society (SABMS) or the Queen of England thought of honouring Olive Doke for her achievements in Lambaland, Paul Kasonga led the fledgling church in Lambaland *on two occasions* – when Doke had been in the mission field for eighteen and twenty-five years – to honour her for her tireless labours among them. Also, Olive Doke wrote the only known biography of Paul Kasonga soon after Kasonga died. She had laboured with him for more than twenty years and in the book she poured out praises for the kind of person Paul Kasonga was.

This researcher says again that we can learn a lot from these two individuals about how missionaries and indigenous people should work together in mutual respect and admiration in the mission field, which, as this researcher hopes to argue in this study, lays a solid foundation for the handover process of pioneer missions work. We can learn even more from the way in which a single missionary woman and a single African man laboured together in a God-honouring way, albeit only for a season, for the crown rights of King Jesus deep in the African jungle.

1.2 Problem Statement

1.2.1 The problem of paternalism and suspicion

It has been observed that one of the most difficult phases to handle in pioneer missions work is the handover process to indigenous leaders. Often relationships between the two parties are marred by paternalism on one hand and an inferiority complex on the other. This has resulted in suspicions from both sides, which has made a conducive working relationship and partnership extremely difficult. This has brought about a lot of heartache and confusion in many church-planting situations. Theoretically, everyone seems to know what to do, but practically, something else seems to happen. In this work, the researcher is suggesting that only where there is mutual respect and admiration from both the pioneer missionaries and the indigenous leaders will we find a handover process that is truly healthy. Therefore, from both sides, this attitude of respect and admiration must be fostered.

So, this study has one particular goal and it is to show how a sensitive handover process in missions can be achieved. We need to learn how to do this from the relationship between Olive Doke and Paul Kasonga so as to minimise the difficulties that are often experienced at this stage of church-planting work.

The work of missions, in its most specific and narrow sense, is not just about spreading the gospel. It is about gathering those who believe the gospel into 'colonies of faith' (i.e. churches that are self-governing, self-sustaining and self-propagating). These churches need to be governed by the very people who have been evangelized. Missions work must have a terminus. Only when the churches are fully governed by the indigenous people can the work of missions be said to be finished in a particular locality. In other words, there needs to come a time when the pioneer missionaries must hand over the work to local leadership.

However, this 'handover' is not an event but a process – a long process – which must be handled sensitively. It begins with the foreign missionaries identifying among the local disciples those who are gifted and growing in grace, and then discipling them into leadership roles. Then it goes into a phase of shared leadership, whereby the converts work as equals with the missionaries in making decisions about God's work. Then, finally, once the missionaries are satisfied that these new leaders can work without them, they withdraw and move on to another sphere of work (or they work under the new leaders, but in a more specialized role – e.g. theological training).

It is often at the stage of shared leadership that biblical norms fail because of the human factor. As already stated, on one hand, there is often a spirit of paternalism on the part of the foreign missionaries; and on the other, there is often a spirit of distrust and an inferiority complex on the part of the local leadership. Sadly, these are often related to money issues. The missionaries hold on to the moneybag and use it as a bit in the mouth of a horse to drive it wherever they wish. In the same way, the local leaders sense this and resent what is happening to the extent that even where there is genuine benevolent charity, it is held suspect. Relationships break down and strangle an otherwise growing work. This has repeated itself over and over again in the story of missions. Thomas Lumba's entire master's thesis is on this subject (Lumba 1995).

1.2.2 The lack of biographies of good role models

There is a secondary need that the researcher hopes to meet by this research. It is that of documenting the biographies of some of our pioneer Baptist leaders in the hope of using these biographies to challenge today's church, especially the Baptist church in Zambia, to rise to the challenge of ongoing pioneer missions work and church planting – using a model of operation that will not repeat the errors of the past, especially with respect to the handover process of the missions work.

The researcher has stated elsewhere (Mbewe 2007, 1) that it is an indictment on the Baptist church in Zambia that one hundred years after the start of this denomination, there is no scholarly and/or popular work on the market covering that illustrious period of its life. There is not a single biography of Olive Doke on the Zambian market (nor is there one in South Africa, the land from where she was sent to Zambia), despite this being thirty-five years after her death. Yet, she was even honoured by the Zambian government and the Queen of England for her outstanding contribution in this part of the world. There is also only one little biographical sketch of the life of Paul Kasonga, written by Olive Doke, soon after he died. There is need for more research after a number of years so as to determine more fully the fruit of his labours. The little research the researcher did for the hundredth anniversary celebrations and his MA thesis, reveals that there were many bright shining lights at that time in history (e.g. Anasi Lupunga, Bob Litana, etc.) and yet they are also almost all forgotten. He is hoping that this research will provide inspiration to others to dig into this rich history and begin unearthing these nuggets of gold for the benefit of a new generation of Christians.

Also, the church in Africa has grown by leaps and bounds in the last one hundred fifty years. Yet this growth is largely in the cities and towns, and south of the Sahara. You only have to go into so many parts of rural Africa and you will find entire villages where nothing more than syncretistic cults flourish. Evangelical Christianity is totally absent. Also, further north, in the Middle East, and into Asia in the northeast, church planting is still very much in its infancy stage because of the antagonism of militant Islam. As stated earlier, experts in missions refer to this region as the 10/40 window. It is the final frontier of missions. It is evident, therefore, from all this that the work of pioneer missions and church planting is far from over.

Educated African Christians need to pay the price of leaving the comforts of the city and go into rural Africa to plant churches that are committed to evangelical Christianity. It will certainly be easier than it was for the likes of Olive Doke who came from a totally different culture. For one, many African professionals going into rural Africa will not need to learn the language because it will probably already be a known language to them. Yet, this is not happening. Exposing today's Christian professionals to the stories of people like Olive Doke may challenge them to consider similar feats for the sake of the gospel and the spreading of God's kingdom. This is why such biographies need to be researched, written, and published.

Uzodinma Obed writes:

> Africa is classified as still having much of the unreached people groups in the world today. The 10/40 window has its largest populated areas in our continent. Apart from this, certain rural areas are yet to be accessed due to their slow response to Western civilisation. All these and more mark Africans as a people with perhaps the greatest need for missions in the entire world . . . What has taken foreign missionaries about two centuries to pursue, can be completed faster if we, the indigenous owners of the work, take it over. Many people are aware of this principle. If Africans will put in half the zeal of the foreigners, our continent will be saved from coast to coast this decade. Let us try it (Obed 2001, 13–14).

The best suited to reach the 10/40 window, which is in the grip of Islam and other Eastern religions, are those of us who are African Christians, and especially those of us who are already practicing some of the professions needed in those countries. Many of these countries are closed to Western missionaries and are very suspicious of Western professionals. However, they are very open to Africans serving there. One reason is simply the fact that we are already on the same continent. We already, therefore, have a lot to do with one another. Granted, there is the challenge of crossing the desert and also of entering into what is largely Arab culture. Yet we need to realise that this challenge is precisely the same as that of pioneer missionaries like Olive Doke when they crossed from urbanized South Africa into the jungle of black central Africa. The fact that a former generation did so and yet today's Christians are largely shunning this task will soon be exposed, as biographies of such people are made more available.

We need to realise, therefore, that the task that lies ahead of us must be overcome, using the very means that God used a century ago to overcome our own spiritual darkness. Therefore, although a lot of the researcher's material is historical, this is not merely a historical study. It is in the context of pastoral theology because this researcher wants to learn from a case study in history how we may do missions and do it better.

1.3 Significance of the Study

In his MA thesis done earlier, this researcher researched the first one hundred years of Baptist history in Zambia and argued for the benefit to church pastors and members if such a history was published and better known. The research did not focus on any individuals nor did it deal in detail with a particular period during that one hundred years. Rather, it was a sweep across the one hundred years in general and merely mentioned key individuals along the way. For the purpose of that thesis, that was adequate.

1.3.1 Moving from the macro-observation to the micro-observation

In this PhD thesis, this researcher is studying two individuals who played very significant roles in the foundation stages of the one hundred years. One of them, Olive Doke, laboured in the country that is now called Zambia for more than half of that period! The researcher is making the move from the study of church history, in a general sense, to the study of Christian biography, in a very specific sense. Putting it slightly differently, he is going from a macro-observation to a micro-observation, so that we can see in more detail the initial building blocks that made up the foundation of that one hundred years history.

One significance of studying the lives of Olive Doke and Paul Kasonga is that today's church will see a very rare example of mutual respect and admiration that produced a strong foundation for Baptist work in Zambia. It helped to produce a handover process from pioneer missionary to indigenous leader that was healthy. If only this would be emulated as we go forward in the unfinished task, as stated earlier, we will avoid falling into the ditches that many have fallen into. It will give a strong foundation to future missions work as today's Christians go forward to plant churches in the needy areas of the world.

The absence of biographies of Zambian Baptist leaders on the Zambian market needs to be redressed. It is about time that Zambian Baptists began to write the biographies of their leaders who have left the field of their labours and gone on to their rest. It is this researcher's hope that his research on the two individuals, Olive Doke and Paul Kasonga, will result in the material being used to produce biographies of the two at a more popular level. This should only be the beginning. More and more such biographies must start coming from the pens of Zambians, in order to challenge today's Christians by the examples of those who have gone before them. The Bible says on this matter: "Remember your leaders, who spoke the word of God to you. Consider the outcome of their way of life and imitate their faith" (Heb 13:7).

As Christians, we should not only learn from church history in general but also from Christian biography in particular.

1.3.2 The effect of good Christian biographies on a later generation

It has been observed by many experts in missions that Africa is being positioned to be the next major source of missionaries in the world. This is the next stage after the unprecedented growth that the church in Africa has experienced in the last century. Nothing is more calculated to produce this missionary zeal than biographies of missionaries. That is what the biographies of David Livingstone and William Carey did to the church in Europe.

A new generation of Christians reading their biographies was challenged to leave their comfort zones in order to take the gospel further afield. In fact, both David Livingstone and William Carey owe their own missionary zeal to the reading of such biographies as that of David Brainerd. John Thornbury notes in his biography of David Brainerd:

> The impact of Brainerd's life on the evangelical missionary vision and Christian enterprise generally has been incalculable. Consider the galaxy of worthy names directly involved in missions who have acknowledged a great debt to the reading of Brainerd's life: John Wesley, Francis Asbury, William Carey, Henry Martyn, Robert Morrison, Samuel Marsden, Christian Frederick Schwartz, David Livingstone, Robert Murray M'Cheyne, Andrew Murray, Sheldon Jackson and Jim Elliot, to name just a few. These people alone were influential in spreading the gospel message to North America, India, Australia, Africa, New Zealand, Palestine, Alaska and South America (Thornbury 1996, 15).

This researcher has little doubt that this will be the effect once biographies of well-known names in Zambian Baptist history begin to be read by a new generation of Christians. Men and women reading the biography of Olive Doke will put aside their excuses of being young and single, or of not being able to leave the comforts of the city, and will go into the harsh rural areas of Africa to take the light of the gospel there. Reading the biography of Paul Kasonga, they will lay aside their excuses of their own inabilities and take up the challenge of providing leadership to fledgling churches in places where the gospel is first having its impact. Those who are involved in church-planting missions will also learn how to sensitively hand over the work of missions to the first local leaders. They will also know what kind of qualifications to look for among those whom they will be considering to take up leadership in the new churches being planted. They will look for spiritual rather than physical qualifications.

In many ways, therefore, this study comes at the right time and is scratching where it is presently itching in the church in Africa, and more specifically, the Baptist church in Zambia, being poised to take up the baton for world missions and evangelization.

1.4 The Hypothesis

The researcher is putting forward a hypothesis, that where mutual respect and mutual admiration are fostered between the missionary and the potential local leaders, the handover process of missions work is likely to go smoothly.

Although respect and admiration have a lot in common and can be used as synonyms, the research is deliberately using both in order to achieve emphasis. By respect he means due regard to a person's feelings and rights, and by admiration he means the recognition of a person's achievement as being unusual and excellent.

1.5 Methodology of the Study

The problem we are seeking to address in this study is how to sensitively handle the handover process from pioneer missionaries to indigenous leaders. The researcher is primarily using an empirical study, using a case study method as his primary data, by looking at the lives of Olive Doke and Paul Kasonga. It is possible to study human relationships in a non-empirical way (e.g. philosophical or conceptual analysis), but such a theoretical approach tends to lack the challenge that says, "It has been done before, and so why can't you do it today?" This is where the case study approach has its advantages. It shows us real human beings doing that which produces the results that we want to produce.

Hendriks argues (referring to Van der Ven):

> Van der Ven (1998, 19–20) calls this type of theology 'empirical theology' because it investigates our empirical reality in order to find credible facts. It explores, describes and explains the empirical aspects of the relations between present-day texts

and contexts. He regards this as most important and necessary, because it provides practical theology with the methods and tools to describe and explain what goes on in the actual lives of actual people . . . and finally to investigate the hypotheses that are formulated with regard to these experiences . . . Without empirical methods and techniques, practical theology runs the risk of generating only rough guesses, naïve associations, subjective projections and unrealistic speculations – in short, of getting stuck in wishful thinking (Hendriks 2004, 212).

However, before we look at the lives of Olive Doke and Paul Kasonga using the case study approach, there are a number of procedures the researcher intends to go through. This road map is meant to finally prove the hypothesis already stated, that where there is mutual respect and mutual admiration, the handover process in missions is smooth.

Firstly, the researcher will review some literature already available on this thorny issue of how pioneer missionaries should sensitively engage in the handover process with the indigenous Christian leaders. This will enable us to see from the history of the church (after the New Testament was written) how so many church leaders have wrestled with this issue. He will also review the few fragments of literature on the lives of Olive Doke and Paul Kasonga for the purpose of showing how little scholarly work has been done on these two important lives in the founding of the Baptist denomination in Zambia.

Secondly, the researcher will do a biblical interpretation of missions. Since he is writing in a context of evangelicalism, where the hermeneutical approach is that of taking the Bible as the divinely inspired authoritative basis of all faith and practice, it is important that he includes an analysis of various biblical passages in order to see what the Bible says about how to phase out pioneer missions work and bring in local leadership. He also hopes this biblical interpretation will show the importance of learning from the lives of leaders who once lived and laboured among us. He trusts that from such an analysis, we can draw lessons that will guide us as we seek to apply the principles we learn from the lives of Olive Doke and

Paul Kasonga to the handover process of pioneer missions work to indigenous leaders.

Thirdly, the researcher will do as thorough a research as possible on the lives of these two individuals. This will make up the greatest part of this research. It will comprise the piecing together of the various fragments that are written about them. More will be available on Olive Doke than on Paul Kasonga partly because she was reporting regularly to the South African Baptist Missionary Society (SABMS), but also because she lived much longer than Paul Kasonga. In order to get more information on the two, as secondary sources, he will also conduct interviews of people who met them and benefited from their ministry. Although these are now few and far between, they are fairly accessible and visiting them for such interviews will be worth the while because these are people who experienced the phenomenon we are talking about.

Fourthly, the researcher will analyse what it was in their attitudes and relationship that made their working together and the handover process to start on such a smooth basis. There must have been a few misunderstandings, but evidence so far seems to show a level of mutual respect and admiration that today's missionaries and indigenous people would do well to emulate.

Finally, the researcher will draw some lessons from the lives of these two individuals (and from the biblical interpretation of missions), which should help today's Christians to do church planting and missions work better. In order to verify these lessons and principles, he will also use a qualitative empirical method and conduct interviews of some Baptist missionaries and indigenous leaders today to hear what their experience has been with respect to the handover process. The fruit of this will be kept as an addendum to this research. Their comments will help to show the relevance of the issues being raised today.

The researcher trusts that the relationship between these two early Christian leaders (Doke and Kasonga) in Baptist work in Zambia will teach all of us how we ought to work with one another in missions. It is his hope that the biographies of Olive Doke and Paul Kasonga will become better known and result in Christians in Zambia and beyond being challenged to take up the mantle these two individuals left behind. He prays that the reading of such biographies will produce a new generation of missionaries and church pastors in Zambia and beyond, who will take the gospel of Jesus Christ to new frontiers so that the knowledge of the glory of God may fill the earth as the water covers the sea!

1.6 Limitations of the Study

There are many ways to learn and be challenged about missions. One would be to do a biblical study so that the foundations of the work of missions are gleaned directly from the pages of the Bible. Another would be a more theological approach, whereby the various issues related to missions (such as the place of the church, the calling of the missionary, the need of the nations, the procedure of church planting, etc.) are investigated and documented. Yet another would be a practical approach, whereby the various components that make up the work of missions (such as human resource, prayer and finances) are studied. Another approach is a more historical one, whereby some section of the history of missions or some biographies of missionaries are studied for the purpose of drawing some significant principles and lessons from there for application today. The researcher has chosen the latter approach – the study of two concurrent biographies – for the reasons given above. By not using the other approaches he has limited the scope of this research. Although he will touch on some biblical content and some theological underpinnings of missions, this will not comprise much of the in-depth study. Also, the practical lessons will be drawn out of the biographical sketches that he hopes to look at, rather than be addressed directly.

Yet even in learning from church history, and Christian biography to be more precise, he has limited himself to one denomination in one country – the Baptist church in Zambia. More lessons would have been learned if his study had involved the pioneer stage of other churches and denominations, both in Zambia and beyond. However, that would have made this study too complex and quite repetitive. He is quite certain that the major lessons to be learned on the subject of his interest will be adequately covered in the one denomination that he has chosen and in the one nation of his interest – Zambia.

Also in learning from Christian biographies of missionaries in Lambaland, he has limited himself to only two. He readily acknowledges that in order to get a fuller picture of the pioneering work in Lambaland, one would need to include in the study a lot more of the pioneering missionaries (e.g. Henry Masters, Arthur Williams, Clement Doke, Arthur Cross, etc.) and a lot more of the early local leaders (e.g. Anasi Lupunga, Bob Litana, etc.). By concentrating on only two individuals, he has limited the examples from whom we are learning. Although this is a limitation, within the scope of this study, the two individuals chosen will prove to be an adequate case study.

Yet another limitation is the amount of data on Paul Kasonga. He died in 1954 – over fifty years ago – and, sadly, the people he left behind who benefited immensely from his ministry were still in the culture of oral tradition. Therefore, going into research on him, the researcher is aware that he will be dependent almost exclusively on oral interviews. Also, most of those interviewed will be secondary sources who would have learned from those among whom Paul Kasonga once laboured. Inevitably, secondary sources are less reliable and need more verification than primary sources. However, it is still best that this work of accumulating data on Kasonga be done now rather than later because even the secondary sources are dying and becoming few and far between. Thankfully, Olive Doke kept commenting on Kasonga when writing in *Lambaland*, and so this will prove to be a good primary source.

1.7 Description of Chapters

1.7.1 Focus of this Research

Chapter 1 gives the direction that this research will take. It will show what this research is all about; namely, the handover process of the work of missions from pioneer missionaries to indigenous leaders. It will also show its nature; namely, a case study of two pioneer leaders of Baptist church history in Zambia. The researcher will show the relevance of the work of missions generally today and why he, in particular, is very interested in this subject. He will introduce the problem of paternalism and suspicion in missions and give his hypothesis for this research. He will end by giving the relevance, procedure and limitations of this study.

1.7.2 Moving from Systems to the Spirit

Chapter 2 will review the relevant literature that deals with the whole subject of the handover process of missions work from pioneer missionaries to indigenous leaders. It will discuss the paucity of literature on this subject and go on to show how those who have, however, dealt with the subject have emphasized the need to move on from mere systems of the church-planting denominations to reliance on the Holy Spirit who is at work in the lives of the converts in the mission field. The researcher will also give an overview of the literature available on the lives of Olive Doke and Paul Kasonga. Thus, it will close with some preliminary conclusions.

1.7.3 The Example of Christ and his Apostles

Chapter 3 is an analysis of pertinent biblical texts on this subject. It will show how the earliest pioneers of the Christian faith went about their own handover process. The chapter will begin with the Lord Jesus Christ himself as he reached the point of handing over the work to his apostles. The chapter will go on to also show how the apostles, as the second line of leaders after the Lord Jesus Christ, also related to those to whom they were to hand over the work of missions. It will close with some pertinent observations from this analysis.

1.7.4 The Lives of Olive Doke and Paul Kasonga

Chapter 4 will be the heart of this research; namely, a biographical sketch of Olive Doke and Paul Kasonga. This chapter will comprise the fruit of all the gleanings from the fragments of the lives of these two individuals that the researcher has been able to put together. Beginning with their childhood days and going on to how both of them found themselves in the same mission station, the researcher will go on to show how they worked together and how, slowly but surely, Olive Doke handed over leadership of the church at the mission station to Paul Kasonga. It will end with the life of Olive Doke after the demise of Paul Kasonga to simply wrap up the biographical sketch.

1.7.5 A True Example of Mutual Respect and Admiration

Chapter 5 will be dedicated to analysing the dynamics of the lives and relationship of Olive Doke and Paul Kasonga. It will start with an effort at understanding the experiences in the background of these two persons that would have prepared them for the kind of relationship that they sustained when they met and worked together. The researcher will then go on to take an in-depth look at the way in which Doke and Kasonga worked together in order to prove his hypothesis. Intermingled with this analysis will be the fruit of the researcher's qualitative empirical work in the form of interviews of current missionaries and indigenous leaders, which also prove the researchers hypothesis, thus showing that what was seen in Doke and Kasonga is the longing of those who are currently on the mission field.

1.7.6 Transforming paternalism into partnership

Chapter 6 will discuss the pertinent lessons to be learned from the Bible and from Doke and Kasonga in order to help us transform the current relationships of paternalism and suspicion that is so common between missionaries and indigenous people into those of mutual respect and admiration. The researcher will use an inductive approach to go from these two role models and propose some theological lessons to learn and some actions to be taken in order to ensure that when the terminus of missions is reached in any mission situation there will be a smooth handover. Again, the researcher's qualitative empirical work in the form of interviews of current missionaries and indigenous leaders will be interwoven into the proposed model to show that it will 'scratch where it is itching'.

1.7.7 Conclusion and final recommendations

Chapter 7 will be the final conclusion to the study. This chapter will summarize the findings of the preceding chapters and provide final recommendations. The researcher will also suggest some work that may still need to be done by way of research in order for the handover process in missions work to be even more seamless for the good of the church in future generations.

CHAPTER 2

Moving from Systems to the Spirit

2.1 Introduction

In this chapter the researcher reviews the relevant literature that deals with the subject of the handover process of missions work from pioneer missionaries to indigenous leaders. The chapter discusses the paucity of literature on this subject and defines some key concepts in this research. It then goes on to show how those who have dealt with the subject of the handover process of missions have emphasized the need to move on from mere suffocating systems of the church-planting denominations to the liberating reliance on the Holy Spirit who is at work in the lives of the converts in the mission field. The researcher also gives a brief bird's-eye view of the literature currently available on the lives of Olive Doke and Paul Kasonga. The chapter closes with some preliminary conclusions.

2.2 The paucity of literature on this subject

This researcher has found that there are not many books and journal articles on the subject of missions tackling to any meaningful depth this all-important area of the handover process of the work of missions to indigenous leaders and the sensitivity that it needs. This researcher's search has found that those books and journals that deal with paternalism in the USA tend to focus on the issue of slavery in the southern states (e.g. Clarke 1975; Nettles 2009; Smylie 1981), while the books and journals that deal with paternalism in South Africa tend to focus on the issue of racism (e.g. England and Paterson 1989; Williams 1995). Then other books and journals tend to deal with this subject as missionaries exercising paternalism over impoverished societies generally and not within the church itself (e.g. Mufuka 1977; Spencer 1982; Jennings 1991; Harries 2008; Lefevere 1985; Jordan 2006). There are even fewer books and journal articles on the lives of Olive Doke and Paul Kasonga.

There are many books on the theology of missions, the call to missions, the nature of missions, the goal of missions, etc. Paul G Hiebert rightly observes, with respect to books on missions that have seen the light of day:

> A generation ago, most books and articles dealt with the nature of God's call, the lostness of humanity, the need for prayer and faithfulness, and the radical challenge of such old customs as widow burning and human sacrifice. Today publications deal with planning, leadership, cultural sensitivity, effective socio-cultural strategies for evangelism, minimizing cultural dislocation in conversion, and how context determines meaning in the contextualization of theology (Hiebert 1994, 9–10).

But there is precious little on the handover of missions by pioneer missionaries to the indigenous people. And yet, this is the terminal of missions in any locality, is it not? The work is not done until the locals own it and run with it successfully.

In the light of the challenges faced by so many mission agencies at this point, it is a wonder that there is so little written about this matter. There are issues that need to be addressed in order for this challenge to be properly redressed. Issues such as cross-cultural communication, an incarnational approach to missions, the contextualization of gospel work, etc., all lie at the back of successful and unsuccessful handover of the work from missionaries to indigenous leaders. Hence, there is enough material for serious research to be done and documented.

Many churches that started very well under foreign missionaries have finally had to split away from them in heart-rending circumstances simply because this stage was not well managed. In certain cases, the foreign missionaries have outlived their welcome. They have overstayed and clung on to leadership for too long. They failed to deal with their converts as equals until it was too late. Sometimes, suspicion on both sides has made working together impossible and a schism has resulted. Thankfully, there have been very good examples of the opposite situation, where mutual respect and admiration has characterized the relationship between foreign missionaries and local leaders. This wholesome relationship has led to benefits that have spurred the church being planted onto higher heights. What can we find in the great plethora of literature on missions about this?

2.3 Some key concepts defined

There are some key concepts around which this research is built and it is important that in this literature review we define them as early as possible. There are essentially three of them.

2.3.1 Missions

Missions may be understood in three senses, as "a participation in the Trinitarian *missio Dei* or mission of God, as the liberating service of the reign of God, and as the proclamation of Jesus Christ as universal Saviour" (Bevans 2012). However, for the purpose of this thesis, missions will be defined as "any effective step taken by a Christian or group of Christians towards fulfilling or enabling the fulfilment of the Great Commission of our Lord Jesus Christ within and *beyond their usual ambit*" (Obed 2001, 15, emphasis mine). Notice that the work of missions must go beyond the sphere in which the church already has a presence. It must go into 'the regions beyond'.

In the *Cape Town Commitment* this ongoing work, which is meant to encompass the earth, is unequivocally stated. "*The church's mission goes on.* The mission of God continues to the ends of the earth and to the end of the world. The day will come when the kingdoms of the world will become the kingdom of our God and of his Christ and God will dwell with his redeemed humanity in the new creation. Until that day, the church's participation in God's mission continues, in joyful urgency, and with fresh and exciting opportunities in every generation including our own" (Birdsall 2010, 5).

Some scholars see a difference between 'mission' and 'missions' and, therefore, use the words differently (e.g. Zulu 2006, 5–7). However, for the purposes of this research, this researcher has used the word 'missions' as referring to all that is involved in carrying out the Great Commission.

This is not easy because it demands our getting out of our comfort zone. It is also not easy because at some stage it must end with the work being handed over to a people to whom it is relatively new to lead it henceforth. It is this work of fulfilling the Great Commission that is the burden of this research. The researcher is using the account of two individuals in the early history of Baptist work in Zambia in order to show how best we can carry this work forward today, especially in sensitively handling the handover process from foreign pioneering missionaries to local Christian leaders. Once we see the price that was paid to bring about the success that we are presently enjoying in Zambia, this information may give us courage to do the same for others. We shall see that it can be done – and that it can be done well!

2.3.2 Partnership

The thinking of this researcher is that there is an important phase in missions work that involves partnership between the pioneer missionaries and the indigenous leadership that is being nurtured to take over the work in due season. Masters, one of the first two missionaries to set up the Kafulafuta Mission (where Olive Doke and Paul Kasonga laboured) acknowledged this when he wrote, "Africa can never be evangelized by the direct effort of the missionary alone. After the pioneering has been done, it is for the missionary to train, inspire, and organize a staff of local evangelists" (Masters 1920, 199). It is this partnership that either suffers due to paternalism (defined below) or is enhanced due to mutual respect and admiration (the heart of this research).

In his fairly exhaustive but concise article entitled 'Partnership' in the *Evangelical Dictionary of World Missions*, Tom A. Steffen shows that there have been at least four views of church-mission relationships: (1) departure, (2) subordination, (3) parallelism, and (4) partnership. In the 'departure', the missionaries leave the mission field once the indigenous leaders are in place and functioning. They may, however, continue to provide financial assistance from a distance. In 'subordination', the missionaries remain with their own independent financial support system, but work under the indigenous leaders. In 'parallelism', the missionaries remain but set up parallel structures, which are totally independent of the indigenous churches and simply cooperate with them in some agreed upon areas. In 'partnership', the missionaries remain and work as equal partners with indigenous leaders.

2.3.3 Paternalism

It is also important to understand the concept of paternalism. This is because, ultimately, it is a paternalistic attitude that fails to treat indigenous leaders as equals in the work of missions that gives birth to most of the problems we find in the handover process. Mikel Neumann says:

> Paternalism, the concept of intervening actively for the perceived wellbeing of another, has long existed in mission. People with knowledge, skills, funds, or power (the older mission) have used them to get new churches to follow their demands. An example of paternalism is a mission keeping control of a work because it feels that the locals are unqualified and would do themselves and the cause of Christ harm by taking leadership. Paternalistic attitudes assume superior knowledge, wisdom and skills. While well intentioned in some cases, they fail to recognize the work of the Holy Spirit in young churches and their leaders (Moreau 2000, 730).

This last point is, in fact, Roland Allen's main point in the book to which we must now turn.

2.4 Missionary Methods – St Paul's or Ours

In his book, *Missionary Methods–St Paul's or Ours*, Roland Allen tackles the question of why missionary work today is not as successful as missionary work done in the days of the apostle Paul in the first century. Although the book has been in print for almost one hundred years (first published in 1912), it still remains in constant demand because it handles such a pertinent issue. Commenting on Roland Allen's overall views in *Missionalia* (33, 3), Dr Philip L. Wickeri wrote:

> Allen had what today might be called a deconstructionist or post-modern understanding of the Christian world mission, a viewpoint that was scandalous for the missionary movement in his time and continues to be problematic for many churches in our own . . . Roland Allen was a missionary enthusiast in the same way that Søren Kierkegaard was a responsible churchman: a prophetic and controversial, theological gadfly who was not taken at all seriously during his lifetime, but whose legacy has been claimed by all strands of the Christian tradition after his death (Wickeri 2005, 482).

Missionary Methods was written by Allen after six years of working as a missionary in China (interspersed by a year or so back in England) when he returned to England to recuperate from a terrible fever which he caught in China. He had experienced the Boxer Uprising first hand. He wrote later in 1927, "I was ill and came home for two years and began to study the methods of the apostle Paul. From that day forward, I began to see light, and gradually as I studied the methods of the apostle, I entered into a large liberty, difficulties were smoothed away, doubts removed, and I began to understand what the establishment of the church might be." Wickeri ended his article on Allen in *Missionalia* by saying, "Allen pioneered in a *via negativa* of witness, a *kenosis* of mission in which self-emptying and empowerment, negation and affirmation, belonged together" (506). It is this phenomenon that this researcher is seeking to emphasize in this thesis – the self-emptying and negation especially on the part of pioneer missionaries phasing into an empowerment and affirmation of the indigenous leaders.

Anyone reading Allen's book soon comes face to face with such questions as, "Is our progress commensurate with all the money and effort expended? Is that progress, if any, as rapid as the work of the church planting by the great apostle? Are we actually planting new churches or merely perpetuating a mission? Are the new causes truly indigenous and self-supporting, and, if not, why not? At what stage in church building does a missionary become dispensable?" (Allen, 1912: v). Relevant to this study is Allen's diagnosis that the major difference between the apostle Paul's approach and ours lies in his trust in the work of the Holy Spirit in those newly converted contrasted with our distrust. Because of this, Paul could entrust the church into the hands of relatively young Christians while he discipled them at a distance.

> St Paul's churches were indigenous churches in the proper sense of the word; and I believe that the secret of their foundation lay in his recognition of the church as a local church (as opposed to our 'national churches') and in his profound belief and trust in the Holy Spirit indwelling his converts and the churches of which they were members, which enabled him to establish them at once with full authority. It is not easy for us today so to trust the Holy Ghost. We can more easily believe in his work in us and through us, than we can believe in his work in and through our converts; we cannot trust our converts to him. But that is one of the most obvious lessons which the study of St Paul's work teaches us (Allen 1991, vii).

Allen observed that,

> in little more than ten years St Paul established the church in four provinces of the Empire: Galatia, Macedonia, Achaia and Asia. Before AD 47 there were no churches in these provinces; in AD 57 St Paul could speak as if his work there was done, and could plan extensive tours into the far west without

anxiety lest the churches which he had founded might perish in his absence for want of his guidance and support (Allen 1991, 3).

He went on to state:

> We have long accustomed ourselves to accept it as an axiom of missionary work that converts in a new country must be submitted to a very long probation and training, extending over generations before they can be expected to be able to stand alone. Today if a man ventures to suggest that there may be something in the methods by which St Paul attained such wonderful results worthy of our careful attention, and perhaps of our imitation, he is in danger of being accused of revolutionary tendencies (Allen 1991, 3–4).

According to Allen, the reason why we delay so much in beginning the handover process is because we have come up with an elaborate system of denominational governance that we cannot allow our converts to rely solely on the Scriptures and the Spirit of God. He writes:

> We cannot imagine any Christianity worthy of the name existing without the elaborate machinery which we have invented. We naturally expect our converts to adopt from us not only essentials, but accidentals. We desire to impart not only the gospel, but the law and the customs . . . St Paul distrusted elaborate systems of religious ceremony, and grasped fundamental principles with an unhesitating faith in the power of the Holy Ghost to apply them to his hearers and to work out their appropriate external expression in them (Allen 1991, 6).

Allen also touches on a matter that certainly needs to be revisited; namely, the use of foreign funds to keep the indigenous people in subjection to the missionaries. This is yet another way in which pioneer missionaries manifest a lack of respect for indigenous people, simply because they are often poorer. He writes:

> Native congregations have before now been held to their allegiance by threats of the withdrawal of pecuniary support. But unity so maintained, by an external bond, is not Christian unity at all. It is simply submission to bondage for the sake of secular advantage and it will fail the moment that any other stronger motive urges in the direction of separation. There is all the difference in the world between gifts freely made by members of the one body to another, as manifestations of the spirit of mutual charity which moves in them, and gifts or subsidies made with the intention of checking freedom of action on the part of the recipients (Allen 1991, 57).

When money is used to leverage submission, the message is evident: the pioneer missionaries are not looking for true biblical partnership in gospel work but simply to maintain superiority. This frustrates true spiritual growth.

A lack of deliberateness in placing emphasis on spiritual rather than financial qualifications can sometimes prolong the handover process because the indigenous people know that a change of leaders may mean a loss of pecuniary benefits. Allen also deals with this. He says:

> The Christians gathered round the [mission] station are very conscious of the advantage of having a European in their midst . . . He can return home and plead for his people with societies and charitably-disposed individuals. He can collect money for his schools and hospitals . . . All these things incline the native converts to prefer a European to a native as the head of their station . . . The native has none of these advantages (Allen 1991, 57–58).

Only a deliberate effort on the part of the pioneer missionaries to show the indigenous people that leadership must not be tied with social or economic means will save the church being planted from such expectations. Sadly, the problem can also be exacerbated by the indigenous leaders' expectations. Allen points this out:

> Moreover, if a native is put in charge of a station, he naturally expects to be paid at the same rate as his white predecessor. If he is not so paid, he feels aggrieved . . . To him the salary for this work, this post, has been fixed at so much, and if he occupies the post he should receive so much (Allen 1991, 58).

That is wrong! A local person should aim to be supported by the indigenous people and not by the external sources that supported the missionaries whose job they have taken over. Hence, their remuneration is likely to reflect that of the local people they will be serving.

Allen also deals with the need to allow the indigenous leaders to take care of future ordinations, once the initial leaders have been chosen by the foreign missionary. He argues that where foreign missionaries perpetuate the monopoly on ordination, they frustrate the sense of responsibility in the indigenous church.

> Where candidates for the ministry are selected by the superior order, where they are ordained solely on the authority of the superior order, and are appointed to their posts by the sole direction of the superior order, those who are so appointed are apt to lose any sense of responsibility to the congregation among whom they minister, and the congregation feels no responsibility for them. The result is an inevitable weakening of what should be the strongest support, both to clergy and laity. Where the superior order consists almost wholly of foreigners, the result is often deplorable. The catechists, teachers, deacons, and priests, so sent out, are wholly independent of the one authority which they really understand, native public opinion; solely dependent upon the one authority which they seldom can understand, the foreign missionary. Consequently they are always striving to act as they think will please the

foreigners, they imitate them as closely as possible, they fear to take any independent action, whilst the members of the congregation on their side feel that they have nothing to do with their appointment. They accept their ministrations so long as they are not seriously offended; they tolerate, but they do not support them, and if anything goes wrong, they disclaim all responsibility (Allen 1991, 100–101).

Again, you cannot fail to see how this undermines true spiritual growth in the churches planted.

Towards the end of his book, Allen passionately expresses his concern about the failure by foreign missionaries to deal with the indigenous people as equal partners in the work of the gospel. He writes:

We have done everything for them. We have taught them, baptized them, shepherded them. We have managed their funds, ordered their services, built their churches, provided their teachers. We have nursed them, fed them, doctored them. We have trained them, and have even ordained some of them. We have done everything for them except acknowledged any equality. We have done everything for them except give place to them. We have treated them as 'dear children', but not as 'brethren' (Allen 1991, 143).

The fact that this was being written by a foreign missionary is incredible, but he must have been grieved by what he was seeing.

If what Allen was concerned about was not evident enough, he went on to show what he had observed:

This attitude is apparent everywhere . . . The moment it is suggested that a council in which natives are in a majority should have the power to direct the action of a white missionary, the moment it is suggested that a native, even though he may be a man of the highest devotion and intellectual ability, should be put into a position of authority in a province where white men still hold office, the white missionaries revolt. They will not hear of such a thing. We acknowledge that the Spirit of God has fitted the man for a position of authority, but he cannot occupy it because we are there (Allen 1991, 143).

As long as this attitude of superiority remains, the churches planted will never truly mature – until all the missionaries retire!

Sometimes it is not an attitude of superiority that leads to this, but a lack of trust that even where the indigenous people are not as mature as the missionaries are in handling the challenges of leadership, God would guide them without the missionaries. Again, Allen is not silent on this matter:

We have imagined ourselves to be, and have acted so as to become, indispensable. In everything we have taught our converts to turn to us, to accept our guidance. We have asked nothing from them but obedience. We have educated our converts to put us in the place of Christ. We believe that it is the Holy Spirit of Christ which inspires and guides us: we cannot believe that the same Spirit will guide and inspire them. We believe that the Holy Spirit has taught us and is teaching us true conceptions of morality, doctrine, ritual: we cannot believe that the same Spirit will teach them . . . It would be better, far better, that our converts should make many mistakes, and fall into many errors, and commit many offences, than that their sense of responsibility should be undermined. The Holy Ghost is given to Christians that he may guide them, and that they may learn his power to guide them, not that they may be stupidly obedient to the voice of authority (Allen 1991, 144–145).

In other words, foreign missionaries should give room for local leaders to make mistakes so that they can learn from them, just as the churches of the foreign missionaries also made mistakes and have grown *because* of those same mistakes.

How successful was Roland Allen in persuading his denomination and his other readers about these views? R. Pierce Beaver in his article entitled "The History of Mission Strategy" in *Perspectives on the World Christian Movement* says,

> he had no followers until after World War II, when missionaries of the faith missions rallied to his position. In essence, his strategy is this: the missionary communicates the gospel and transmits to the new community of converts the simplest statement of the faith, the Bible, the sacraments and the principle of ministry. He then stands by as a counselling elder brother while the Holy Spirit leads the new church, self-governing and self-supporting, to develop its own forms of polity, ministry, worship and life. Such a church is spontaneously missional (Beaver 2009, 238).

2.5 Transforming Mission – Paradigm Shifts in Theology of Mission

Bosch also briefly addressed this matter in *Transforming Mission – Paradigm Shifts in Theology of Mission*. He certainly saw the issues that concerned Roland Allen eighty years earlier. He wrote:

> In theory, Protestant missions aimed at the establishment of 'independent' younger churches. The pervasive attitude of benevolent paternalism, however, often militated against this declared goal. The enthusiastic discussions about 'self-governing, self-expanding, and self-supporting churches', so prominent around the middle of the nineteenth century, were, for all practical purposes, shelved by the beginning of the twentieth. The younger churches had, almost unnoticed, been demoted from churches in their own right to mere 'agents' of the missionary societies . . . They were churches, yes, but of a lesser order than those the West, and they needed benevolent

control and guidance, like children not yet come of age (Bosch 1991, 369–370).

It is worth noting that it was exactly in the period mentioned by Bosch – the beginning of the twentieth century – when individuals like Olive Doke showed the opposite attitude to that which had become commonplace in the mission field. And Bosch is not the only one to put a label on this era as an era of paternalism. Bosch makes the point that it is easy to use nice-sounding platitudes when you have emptied them of their meaning at a practical level. Many Western missionaries tended to be guilty of this when it came to sharing leadership with indigenous Christians.

Bosch goes further and points to two areas that caused this to be the case at the turn of the nineteenth into the twentieth century. He writes:

> First, there was the problem that early converts often came from the fringes of society and were the poorest of the poor. So the missionaries had to develop industries in order to make converts economically independent . . . Such a policy makes the missionary an employer and the Indian or African Christian an employee, and easily destroys awareness of the fact that they are, first and foremost, sisters and brothers to each other (Bosch 1991, 370).

In other words, what was meant to help the converts in the end became a snare to them and hindered their growth into full maturity and responsibility.

Bosch gives the second cause as the foreign structures imposed on the indigenous churches.

> The second difficulty lay in the fact that the churches on the 'mission field' were structured on exactly the same lines as those on the missionaries' home front, where a completely different socio-economic system obtained. The results were often disastrous. A study group which visited India in 1920 declared, 'We have created conditions and methods of work which can only be maintained by European wealth' (quoted

by Gilhuis 1955, 60). . . . Willy-nilly the Western mission agencies taught their converts to feel helpless without money (Bosch 1991, 370–371).

In order for local Christians to take full responsibility of their situation, the tools of the trade must be such that they can sustain them without external support. Gospel partnership can still continue but benevolent paternalism must stop!

As Bosch comes to the end of his survey of the twentieth century, he still sees this paralyzing effect of paternalism. He writes:

> The new mood was not free from paternalism. Forgotten were the pleas of Rufus Anderson and others for allowing younger churches and 'new' nations to stand on their own and develop along lines of their own choice. More generally than was the case in the previous century, missionaries from the West viewed peoples of the Third World as inferior to themselves and not really to be trusted with the future of the church (Bosch 1991, 379).

Ultimately, this is the issue. It is whether nationals can be fully trusted or not. Allen was right when he said that the answer to that question depends on our view of the work of the Holy Spirit in the hearts of our converts.

Thus at the beginning of the twenty-first century, the cry to do away with paternalism is even louder. In the *Cape Town Commitment*, this cry is heard afresh: "We urgently seek a new global partnership within the body of Christ across all continents, rooted in profound mutual love, mutual submission, and dramatic economic sharing without paternalism or unhealthy dependency. And we seek this not only as a demonstration of our unity in the gospel, but also for the sake of the name of Christ and the mission of God in all the world" (Birdsall 2010, 17).

2.6 A review of other relevant literature

Moreau, Corwin and McGee have recently written a very good primer on missions entitled *Introducing World Missions – A Biblical, Historical and Practical Survey* (2004). The authors admit that their work is only introductory. However, they deal with the subject of this thesis in at least two places. First, they say of the beginning of the twentieth century:

> Although Christianity by now had become the first religious faith to become a world religion, the centre of gravity remained in the northern hemisphere, missionaries travelled on a one-way street from Europe and America to the non-Christian world, and paternalism (the practice of controlling others by acting like a parent without giving them responsibility for themselves) too frequently marked their posture toward indigenous leaders (Azariah 1910, 315). (Moreau et al. 2004, 136–7)

Second, they talk about partnerships.

> The word *partnership* has reached the status of a buzzword in mission circles today. Creating and carrying out partnerships in which each member is valued and has something to offer to the partnership is difficult under the best of circumstances. This is especially true when the partnering organizations are from different cultures and have widely differing management and organizational structures and styles. The difficulties are magnified when one of the partners brings the bulk of the necessary financial resources, as is most often the case when Western churches or missions partner with churches or missions from the southern hemisphere. It requires strong relationships and wise, godly interaction for the partnership to be genuine and for all partners to feel that they are on an equal footing (Moreau et al. 2004, 286).

Moreau, et al, quote Daniel Rickett, the long-time director of partner development for Partners International, who lists seven mistakes that partners often make (2004, 286–287). This researcher merely lists them down here without any amplification, which can be found by referring to the book:

Mistake 1: Assuming you think alike.

Mistake 2: Promising more than you can deliver.

Mistake 3: Taking to the road without a map.

Mistake 4: Underestimating cultural differences.

Mistake 5: Taking shortcuts.

Mistake 6: Forgetting to develop self-reliance.

Mistake 7: Running a race with no end.

These mistakes are often made at a personal level and then they take on institutional significance simply because the individuals who make the mistakes represent partnering organizations. The point being made by Rickett is that partnership can be destroyed even when the two parties mean well for each other, simply because they took too many things for granted. Care and sensitivity must be woven into partnerships to avoid heartaches. We shall see how this worked itself out in the case study we are looking at in this thesis.

In his article on "Foreign Financing of Indigenous Workers" in the *Evangelical Dictionary of World Missions*, Charles Bennett shows the various stages that this whole process has gone through over the years. He points out that nineteenth-century missionaries tended to employ local evangelists and pastors but soon noticed the dependency syndrome that this created. They then reacted to the opposite extreme and in the first half of the twentieth century many insisted that no funding should go from Western countries into the Majority World to pay or subsidize local evangelists and pastors. Bennett showed that in the second half of the twentieth century a partnership seems to have developed whereby Western funding agencies are paying for the support of many indigenous workers. This has had its challenges. He raises two questions that have had to be addressed:

1. How can you give them financial assistance without creating unhealthy dependency?

2. How can you assure financial accountability and proper use of funds if you have no direct control over them?

He gives some answers to these two questions, providing a sense of direction rather than complete solutions. For the purpose of this thesis, this researcher's interest is in his final statement: "The key to success is to have open trust relationships in a partnership between equals" (Moreau et al. 2004, 365–366). Again, this researcher's thesis is that this does not start when money is about to exchange hands. It must be an attitude that must be cultivated with time and must already be there between the two parties by the time systems are being put in place to ensure accountability. It is this sensitivity that this researcher is advocating for.

Although this article is primarily about institutional partnerships, its principles apply initially to interpersonal partnerships before they become institutional. For instance, Steffen writes:

> A common vision serves as the driving force behind effective strategic partnerships. Partners . . . agree upon assigned roles and rules that foster complimentary participation . . . Fundamental to the success of any strategic partnerships is trust. Open communication facilitates trust building and efficiency (Moreau et al. 2004, 727).

This researcher cannot put it any better. These are the issues that must be emphasized in interpersonal relationships in order to foster partnerships that will result in long-term benefits in the work of missions.

Bill Taylor (Moreau et al. 2004, 376) brings out this personal nature of sustained and fruitful partnerships by pointing out four areas that cause them to work.

> (1) **Initiative with relationship:** Partnerships work when they form after sustained trust and relationship building, not simply because someone has a passion and rushes unto the organizational marriage to get the job done. (2) **Cross-cultural wisdom:** Partnerships work when cultural differences are understood. Some leaders, operating with their mono-cultural framework of values and behaviour, end up imposing themselves, subconsciously regarding their partners as junior, or secondary, players. (3) **Common goals:** Partnerships work

when there is a commitment to common objectives. Then partners can celebrate how much they truly need each other and focus on fruitfulness. **(4) Accountability and evaluation:** Partnerships work when cultivated and strengthened by monitoring ventures for effectiveness. We can make changes before losing friendships.

One of the benefits of true partnership in missions between pioneer missionaries and local leaders is in addressing syncretism. Syncretism is a blind spot that needs an outsider to notice. Yet, that outsider needs to have a wholesome relationship with the local leaders, if they (the local leaders) are going to address it. Otherwise, they tend to simply react negatively to the missionary for pointing it out and insisting that all syncretistic activities and associations must be abandoned. However, where the missionary is in a relationship of trust and mutual respect with the local leaders, they will take up the matter themselves and champion it with their people.

Moreau refers to this in his article on "Syncretism" in the *Evangelical Dictionary of World Missions*. He writes:

> Because of the convoluted nature of culture, the declaration of syncretism in a particular setting cannot be simply left in the hands of expatriate missionaries. The local community must be empowered to biblically evaluate their own practices and teachings. Missionaries must learn to trust that indigenous peoples are able to discern God's leading and trust God to develop and maintain biblically founded and culturally relevant FAITH and PRAXIS in each local context. Finally, Christians of every culture must engage in genuine partnerships with Christians of other cultures, since often the outsider's help is needed to enable local believers, blinded by culture and familiarity, to see that which contravenes scriptural adherence to the first commandment (Moreau 2004, 294–295).

Before we become too negative about paternalism, it needs to be said that the very first stage of missions work invariably has to be paternalistic. We shall see this in the example of the Lord Jesus Christ and his apostles. This is because at that stage, the missionaries are the sole custodians of biblical truth. They need to pass it on. However, at some stage in the process a relationship of equal partners must commence. Again, this is evident from the example of Christ and his apostles. Ralph D. Winter seems to see this two-phased approach in missions work. The early and new mission work is pioneering and inevitably paternalistic. The later and more advanced work is the one that involves partnering and participation (Winter 2009, 271). It is the failure to properly handle the transition from the first to the second phase that often dogs the work of missions in the world.

The researcher ends this section of the literature review with just one more citation. It is pertinent to this research by its sharpness in condemning the paternalistic attitude of the earlier missionaries. R. Pierce Beaver says that,

> mission executives and field missionaries took the colonial-ist view that Africans were inferior and therefore could not provide ministerial leadership . . . Paternalism – treating the native church as young children – stunted their development. All missions were paternalist and colonialist at the turn of the century (Moreau et al. 2009, 235–236).

It is "at the turn of the century" that our story of Olive Doke and Paul Kasonga is found. That is why it is such a refreshing story. At a time when missionaries saw Africans as inferior and when "all missions were paternal-ist and colonialist", what is it that made Olive Doke so different?

2.7 A Quest for Authentic Practice of Missions in Africa

Getting closer home (i.e. in Zambia), Thomas Lumba wrote a thesis for his Bachelor of Divinity degree in 1995 in which he dealt with conflicts be-tween missionaries and local leaders using the Southern Baptists in Zambia as a case study. He entitled it *A Quest for Authentic Practice of Missions in Africa*. Everything he saw as wrong, and which led to the breakdown of relations between the Baptist missionaries and the local leaders, would not have happened if the example of Olive Doke and Paul Kasonga had been followed. For instance, he stated:

> Some foreign missionaries have found it more convenient to be much closer to their Western counterparts on their mission fields than to their African brothers and sisters of the same faith. In the Zambian conflict of the Baptist missionaries and the national leaders over the issue of work permits, which we shall discuss later as a case study, the former relied more heavily on the advice from the embassy officials and their secular lawyers than on seeking more open and reconciliatory contacts with their national 'opponents'! (Lumba 1995, 14).

Although Lumba speaks about the Baptist Mission of Zambia and the Baptist Convention of Zambia being partners, he later acknowledges that their form of partnership was a parallelism and not a true partnership. The two maintained parallel structures that were totally autonomous and only cooperated in a number of joint ventures. In fact, part of the cause of their crisis lay in this very fact. The mission never handed over the tools of the ministry, but held onto them in a parallel structure. Lumba quotes George W. Peters who says:

> To the question of who is to manage the office of the administration, this should go into the hands of the church at the earliest possible date. Here indigenization should begin. There is no scriptural, historical or practical reason for a dual administration in a field where a church of like persuasion and common loyalty exists, especially a church which is the result of the mission's effort (Lumba 1995, 32).

Lumba handles a number of institutional causes that lead to conflict between pioneering missionaries and indigenous leaders – issues like policy decisions, personal lifestyles, and finances. What he deals with in each of these areas is certainly serious food for thought. For the purpose of this book, the researcher goes straight to personal lifestyles. There he deals with the affluent lifestyles, ethnocentric attitudes and complexes malaise of the missionaries. In the latter, he speaks about the inner personal problems some missionaries struggle with to adapt to their new home country, their new people and to the customs of their new setting. With a superiority complex, they tend to look at Africans as 'raw savages'. Under the complexes malaise, Lumba also deals with the inferiority complex that often characterizes the national leaders, making them think they can never do what the missionaries are able to do. Thus, whatever the missionaries say is superior.

> The missionary, with a superiority complex, and the national, with an inferiority complex, are teamed to work together in a mission-church partnership. Two such different minds are required to sit together around a table, making decisions for the growth of God's work in the churches and for building relationships. It would be foolish and illogical to close our eyes and pretend that in the name of Christianity there could be equality (Lumba 1995, 45).

Or as Willem Saayman puts it with respect to missions in the Dutch Reformed Church, "Apart from ethnocentrism, cultural differences and unequal socio-economic power relations, one important root of this problem has been the persistent belief that black people are somehow inferior beings, in some way representative of the threatening darkness of evil" (Saayman 2001, 477). A good example of this is the reference to the Africans by Bishop Knight-Bruce in his *Memories of Mashonaland* as "a collection of babies in moral questions, who don't know their right hand from their left, and who have no power of self-control" (Knight-Bruce 1989, 171).

Lumba's conclusion, therefore, is both painful and correct:

> We can conclude that there is very little evidence of real partnership between foreign missionaries and indigenous Christians as far as Baptist missions work is concerned. Instead, partnership as practiced seems to be very close to the parallelism and dichotomy model. There exists an unbalanced relationship of

the wealthy, powerful Western mission agencies on the one hand and the financially poor African churches on the other. We concur with Mbiti that this 'partnership' has been largely a cover-up for a continued paternalistic relationship between the so-called partners (Lumba 1995, 51).

My single criticism of Lumba's thesis is his failure to address the question of attitude in both the foreign missionaries and the indigenous leaders when he comes to give his solution. The reason why systems fail is because there are wrong attitudes in the persons who either come up with the systems or who carry out those systems. Whereas Lumba sees this as part of the problem, he fails to deal with it in his solution. He merely urges African churches to take the work of missions seriously – and, as far as that is concerned, he is right. However, if the issue of attitudes is not dealt with, the African church will merely repeat the errors of the foreign missionaries when they also become foreign missionaries wherever they will go. This researcher is more in favour of the final appeal of Mulemfo in his well-written article on Swedish missionaries in Africa. He writes:

> What we need is a paradigm shift in the understanding of missionary work in Africa and of the presence of expatriate missionaries. African church leaders have a vital responsibility in this, to reconsider mission as a complementary endeavour. I want to suggest again that to make the concept of complementarity successful, the older and younger churches should strive to review their previous attitudes to one another. They need to try and build an environment conducive to reconciliation, repentance, forgiveness, fellowship, service, proclamation, and dialogue. These qualities would play an important role in their common missionary endeavour and would demonstrate their oneness in Jesus Christ (Mulemfo 2001, 18).

What Lumba failed to see in the relationship between foreign missionaries and indigenous Christians among the Southern Baptists in Zambia is in fact what we see illustrated in this book in the example of Olive Doke and Paul Kasonga (i.e. the trust in the work of the Holy Spirit, and hence the bringing into leadership of Paul Kasonga fairly early in his Christian life). However, before we go on to look at this refreshing example, let us turn to the Holy Scriptures and learn from there what the biblical relationship should be like between the foreign missionary and the indigenous leadership.

2.8 Literature on Doke and Kasonga

Piecing together the lives of Olive Doke and Paul Kasonga was not a straightforward process because of the paucity of major works on the two individuals. This is despite the foundational roles that the two played in the establishment of the Baptist church in Zambia. However, the sources that the researcher found were fairly adequate for the purpose of this research.

The most important of all the sources was the *Lambaland* newsletter, which the missionaries in Lambaland maintained throughout the period under review. This newsletter was produced quarterly and documented the major events that were taking place on the mission field. Whereas Paul Kasonga never contributed any article to this newsletter, he was often mentioned during the period of his leadership until his death in 1954. As for Olive Doke, she penned many of the reports and so shared with her readership what God was doing in her life and ministry while she was in Lambaland. This is a vital primary source and so the researcher gleaned as much as he could from its contents. The fruit of his gleanings make up an important part of his biographical chapter on Olive Doke and Paul Kasonga.

There are two important biographies of both Olive Doke and Paul Kasonga, and Olive Doke wrote both of them. The first is an autobiography, written in 1964. This remains unpublished and a copy of it is in the Baptist Archives in South Africa. The second is a biography that Olive Doke wrote of Paul Kasonga in 1955, a year after he died. It is entitled, *Paul the Leper – Apostle to the Lambas*. The South Africa Baptist Missionary Society published this. It contains the most authentic and comprehensive information on the life of Paul Kasonga because the one person who spent the greatest amount of time labouring alongside him wrote it. The fact that it was published and circulated among the very people to whom he ministered meant that if there were any major errors they would have been pointed out. The researcher has not come across anything to suggest that this was the case.

Clement Doke, Olive's brother, wrote a biographical sketch of his time in Lambaland, entitled, *Trekking in South Central Africa 1913–1919*. Although this book is primarily about his own life, during the relatively short period he laboured in Lambaland, it also contains valuable biographical material on both Olive Doke and Paul Kasonga, covering the first few years of their association with Kafulafuta Mission. It is an important primary source for anyone wanting to write about these two individuals.

Louise Kretzschmar (1996) wrote on Olive Doke entitled, *Olive Carey Doke: A Neglected Baptist Pioneer*. As far as its biographical content is concerned, there is much to commend the document. However, she was trying to prove a point that could not really be sustained. Her argument in that thesis basically challenged the Baptist Union of South Africa as to why they could support a woman preaching to black Africans in Northern Rhodesia but refuse to accept women preachers in Baptist churches in South Africa. She considered that to be hypocritical on their part. This researcher posits that her thesis was unsustainable because data from his own research shows that whereas Olive Doke played a major teaching and preaching role in the first phase of her missionary work, when the indigenous leaders were nurtured in the church on the mission field, she took a few steps backwards and let them do the preaching and the teaching. It is evident that she saw her role in the latter years as one of encouragement and discipling the men in the background. Even when she was invited to sit in for their leadership meetings, she elected to be quiet unless specifically asked to comment. So, as important a source of data on Olive Doke as this document may have been, its thesis is yet to be proven.

Apart from the sources mentioned above, there were a few magazine articles (Doke 1966; Jennings 1965; etc.) that the researcher came across. These were written towards the end of Olive Doke's life and well after her retirement (which took place in 1959). They contain reflections on her ministry after being in Lambaland for about fifty years. They do not provide new data but rather show the satisfaction she had in seeing the fruit of her labours, as her successors – the indigenous leaders – were now carrying on the work that she had helped to start. That is important for the purpose of this research because it confirms that there was a successful handover process. This researcher wanted to see what it was that made this process successful.

2.9 Conclusion

It is evident from the foregoing that there is paucity of literature on the subject of the sensitive handover of missions from pioneer missionaries to indigenous leaders (and especially literature on Olive Doke and Paul Kasonga). However, those who have addressed this matter have been largely concerned about the ongoing presence of paternalism on the mission field and its negative effect on the process towards indigenization. The ongoing presence of paternalism has been largely due to the missionaries' trust in their complicated systems and structures rather than upon the work of the Holy Spirit in the lives of the new indigenous leaders. In a secondary way, it has also been due to the failure by indigenous leaders to thrive in true spirituality so as to gain the confidence and admiration of pioneer missionaries.

Money has often been a leverage that missionaries have used to keep indigenous leaders in subjection to them and this has also been a cause of much suspicion and acrimony from indigenous leaders. Instead of missionaries emphasizing spirituality, they wait for indigenous leaders to also qualify financially before they can be true equals. Indigenous leaders have detested this. Hence, even the final choice and ordination of leaders still remains in the hands of the missionaries long after the first indigenous leaders have been chosen. Sadly, the inferiority complex on the part of indigenous leaders only exacerbates this situation.

Hence, it is evident from the foregoing, that the search for true partnerships between new indigenous leaders and pioneer missionaries is still going on. There are some success stories around the world. It is incumbent upon us to study them and learn as much as we can from them. It is the goal of this researcher to do just that by studying the example of Olive Doke and Paul Kasonga.

CHAPTER 3

The Example of Christ and His Apostles

3.1 Introduction

In this chapter, the researcher analyzes pertinent biblical texts on the subject of the sensitive handover process of missions work from pioneer missionaries to indigenous church leaders. He recognizes from the very onset that not all Bible scholars would agree with his findings because there are many hermeneutical approaches to the Bible. He also thinks that it is beyond the purpose of this study to justify his approach but merely to identify it. Yet for the purpose of his research, he finds the approach that he uses to be most suitable.

Hermeneutically, the researcher approaches this chapter from a faith perspective. From such a perspective, Scripture is what motivates practice in general and missions in particular. Christopher J. H. Wright (2006, 22) writes, "The reason why we know we should be doing mission, the basis, foundation or grounds on which we justify it, must be found in the Bible. As Christians, we need a biblical basis for everything we do." Or as John R. W. Stott (Stott 1990, 11) puts it, "But can we leap the gap of nineteen centuries between the apostles and us, and apply the Acts text to ourselves without manipulating it to suit our own preconceived opinions? Yes, it is right to affirm that the Word of God is always relevant."

It also needs to be stated that this biblical analysis is relevant to the study not only to serve the interests of the researcher and his group of churches but also because of the case study that will follow. Olive Doke and Paul Kasonga were in the same Baptist tradition, which had a similar

hermeneutical approach to the Bible. Thus in including this biblical interpretation of missions we are seeking to understand how these two individuals understood missions and why they thought the handover process ought
to take place in this way at its terminus.

This chapter will show how the earliest pioneers of the Christian faith
went about their own handover process. It will begin with the Lord Jesus
Christ himself as he reached the point of handing over the work to his
apostles. The chapter will go on to also show how the apostles, as the second line of leaders after the Lord Jesus Christ, also related to those to whom
they were to hand over the work of missions. It is hoped that the thread
of mutual respect and admiration will be noticed in the analysis. Finally,
this chapter will close with some pertinent observations from this analysis.

3.2 The church's first missionaries

The challenge of sensitively handing over the product of missions – the local churches – to indigenous leadership is one that started in Bible times.
To begin with, the Lord Jesus Christ himself knew that there was a terminus to his work on earth. Preparing for that terminus involved the preparation of twelve apostles so that upon his death, resurrection and ascension,
they would be ready to take the work forward. It is important for us to see
how he did that and to learn from him as we seek to do the same in our
work of mission today.

Also in the Bible we have the opportunity to see the church's first missionaries – the apostles – as they worked towards their own terminus in the
work of church planting that they were engaged in right across Asia Minor
and Europe. They also knew that they had to work towards a terminus.
This terminal point could only be reached as they prepared leaders for the
churches they were planting and handed over the churches to them. Again,
we must look at how they sensitively and maturely engaged in this process.

As we analyse the work of the Lord Jesus Christ and his apostles, we
could use the three stages that Bruce suggests missions work goes through
before it reaches its terminal stage: (1) the initial paternalistic phase, (2) the

shared leadership phase, and (3) the final withdrawal phase.[1] Bruce noted this three-staged approach in the work of the Lord Jesus Christ when he wrote, "These twelve, however, as we know, were to be something more than travelling companions or menial servants of the Lord Jesus Christ. They were to be, in the mean time, students of Christian doctrine, and occasional fellow-labourers in the work of the kingdom, and eventually Christ's chosen trained agents for propagating the faith after he himself had left the earth" (1988, 30). In the first phase, they were to be students of Christian doctrine. In the second phase, they were to be fellow labourers in the work of the kingdom. And in the third phase, they were to propagate the faith after he himself had left the earth. It is these three phases that this researcher will use as broad brackets into which to divide the work of the Lord Jesus Christ and that of his apostles in sensitively handing over the work of missions to their successors. The growing sense of equality and admiration is unmistakable, especially as the apostles gave way to the new leaders emerging under them.

Hence, the study of relevant biblical texts is our next task, before we look at the example of Olive Doke and Paul Kasonga. This study will act as a backdrop for us to examine the handover process that took place between these two individuals in Baptist history in Zambia so that we can arrive at a truly biblical analysis of their work. It is from this analysis that we can then see how we should emulate them.

3.3 The Example of Jesus

The best place to begin when considering the subject of the sensitivity required for a wholesome handover process from missionaries to indigenous leaders is the example of Jesus – the missionary par excellence! When Jesus began his public ministry, he not only evangelized but also handpicked a few men that he was to groom into the first leaders of the church. The Bible says:

---

1. More is said about these stages of missions work later in this thesis. For now it is sufficient that the phases are listed down.

In these days he went out to the mountain to pray, and all night he continued in prayer to God. And when day came, he called his disciples and chose from them twelve, whom he named apostles: Simon, whom he named Peter, and Andrew his brother, and James and John, and Philip, and Bartholomew, and Matthew, and Thomas, and James the son of Alphaeus, and Simon who was called the Zealot, and Judas the son of James, and Judas Iscariot, who became a traitor (Luke 6:12–16).

3.3.1 The Initial Paternalistic Phase

In the first stage of Jesus' ministry, he largely taught all the people everywhere he went. He was an itinerant preacher. Even when his ministry was largely successful in one place, he still insisted that they move on so that he could preach elsewhere too (e.g. Mark 1:32–33). He knew that he had the truth and he needed to share it with the people in Galilee, Nazareth, etc. Although he chose his disciples very early in his public ministry, they initially functioned more as his students and helpers, rather than as individuals to whom he could entrust any teaching or leadership roles.

It has been rightly observed that Jesus chose "a band of poor illiterate Galilean provincials, utterly devoid of social consequence" (Bruce 1988, 37). His twelve apostles largely comprised obscure fishermen, tax collectors and zealots. None of them were rabbis, rulers, or rich men. They had neither great education, nor great possessions, nor great titles. They were crude, unlearned and humble men. These men were simple and sincere. In other words, from the very beginning, Jesus must have known that he had his work cut out for him. These were the men he was to train to take his message to the ends of the earth. This is often the lot that missionaries have to develop into church leaders because where pioneer missions work takes place you will often find that the people are still largely uncivilized. Civilization tends to often be a product of the establishment of the Christian faith.

Mark tells us that these men were to "be with him and [that] he might send them out to preach and have authority to cast out demons" (Mark 3:14–15). The reference to being with him suggested an intense period of education for them. They were to learn from Jesus, both by precept and by example, over a period of no less than three years. It was to be the most life-changing experience that they were to go through as they saw Jesus in every aspect of his life and heard all his teachings. Referring to the need for this "being with Jesus", Bruce asserts:

> In the training of the twelve for the work of the apostleship, hearing and seeing the words and works of Christ necessarily occupied an important place. Eye and ear witnessing of the facts of an unparalleled life was an indispensable preparation for future witness-bearing. The apostles could secure credence for their wondrous tale only by being able to preface it with the protestation: "That which we have seen and heard declare we unto you." None would believe their report, save those who, at the very least, were satisfied that it emanated from men who had been with Jesus (Bruce 1988, 41).

Warren W. Wiersbe (1987, 34) says:

> Jesus spent all night in prayer before choosing these twelve men (Luke 6:12). When he selected them, he had three purposes in mind: (1) training them by personal example and teaching, (2) sending them out to preach the gospel, and (3) giving them authority to heal and cast out demons. (See Mark 1:14–15, 38–39; 6:7–13.) These twelve men would thus be able to continue his work when he returned to the Father, and they would also be able to train others to carry on the ministry after them (2 Tim 2:2).

3.3.2 The Shared Leadership Phase

From the teaching ministry of Jesus it is evident that somewhere along the way, his emphasis changed from teaching the general populace together with his disciples to concentrating on teaching his disciples only. An example of this can be seen in that the first extended sermon of his is the Sermon on the Mount (Matt 5–7), while the last extended sermon of his is the Upper Room Discourse (John 13–17). In the first sermon, he was addressing the populace together with his disciples. In the last sermon, he was only addressing his twelve disciples behind closed doors. These were to be his successors and so he was now giving them undivided attention.

They were to be sent out to preach and to cast out demons, just as he had been doing. In other words, their training was to involve a lot of practical works even before Jesus finally handed over the work to them. Hence, on a number of occasions he paired them up and sent them on evangelistic trips (Luke 10:1). In that context they learnt to work together and to see the power of God at work despite their human frailties. They were so excited about this that Jesus had to caution them on one occasion. He said, "Behold, I have given you authority to tread on serpents and scorpions, and over all the power of the enemy, and nothing shall hurt you. Nevertheless, do not rejoice in this, that the spirits are subject to you, but rejoice that your names are written in heaven" (Luke 10:19–20). He wanted them to have the right attitude to their newly acquired supernatural powers.

Bruce says about these twelve:

> From the time of their being chosen, indeed, the twelve entered on a regular apprenticeship for the great office of apostleship, in the course of which they were to learn, in the privacy of an intimate daily fellowship with their Master, what they should be, do, believe, and teach, as his witnesses and ambassadors to the world. Henceforth the training of these men was to be a constant and prominent part of Christ's personal work. He was to make it his business to tell them in darkness what they should afterwards speak in the daylight, and to whisper in their ears what in after years they should preach upon the housetops (Bruce 1988, 30).

3.3.3 The Final Withdrawal Phase

Finally, a time was to come when Jesus was to hand over the keys of the kingdom to them. This was the terminal point for Jesus' earthly ministry. Just before he went to the cross he prayed to the Father, saying, "I glorified you on earth, having accomplished the work that you gave me to do . . .

I have manifested your name to the people whom you gave me out of the world . . . For I have given them the words that you gave me, and they have received them and have come to know in truth that I came from you; and they have believed that you sent me" (John 17:4–8). Kostenberger (2004, 491) says, "'I have given them the words you gave me' sums up the result of Jesus' three-year teaching ministry among his disciples." Jesus only felt that his work on earth was finished when he had given to the first leaders of the church the truths that he had come with from heaven. It is important for us to notice the attitude that he exemplified in the process of doing so.

Though Jesus was the Son of God, he came down to the level of his disciples and treated them as if he was truly at their level. Hence, one aspect of Jesus' life that was totally mind-blowing was his humility. He was a good role model for servanthood and partnership. We see him exemplify servanthood in John 13 when he washed his disciples' feet. He said to his disciples:

> Do you understand what I have done to you? You call me Teacher and Lord, and you are right, for so I am. If I then, your Lord and Teacher, have washed your feet, you also ought to wash one another's feet. For I have given you an example, that you also should do just as I have done to you. Truly, truly, I say to you, a servant is not greater than his master, nor is a messenger greater than the one who sent him. If you know these things, blessed are you if you do them (John 13:12–17).

The washing of the feet of guests in a home in Jewish culture was the work of the lowest servant or slave in the household. This was necessary because walking in sandals was the most common form of movement, and this inevitably caused people to arrive at their destinations with dirty and dusty feet. Part of hospitality was 'the washing of feet" because it enabled guests to settle down more comfortably. The master of the house never washed the feet of his guests. It was the work of the lowest servant or slave. Yet on this occasion, the Lord Jesus – the Teacher and Lord – washed the feet of his disciples. Among the many reasons he gave was that he wanted to give an example to his disciples so that, long after he was gone, they would do the same to one another.

This does not mean we Christians today are to literally wash one an-other's feet (though some churches do that). However, in the church, we are to do the lowest and most menial work for one another, despite the sta-tion we occupy in the context of Christian leadership. This must also apply in the relationship between missionaries and indigenous leaders. Surely, if Jesus was the master, and yet he stooped low enough to be the chief ser-vant among them, no one should be too high to be a servant among God's people – not even missionaries. It is this humble spirit, which will make a missionary enter into a shared leadership with indigenous people. It is also this humble spirit, which will make him take a few steps backwards and let them lead him in the last phase of the missions work.

Bruce notes:

> Is not the morality here enjoined indeed rare? Are not the vir-tues called into play by acts of condescension and charity most high and difficult? Who dreams of calling them easy? How ut-terly contrary they are to the native tendencies of the human heart! How alien from the spirit of society! Is it the way of men to be content with the humblest place, and to seek their felicity in serving others? Doth not the spirit that is in us lust unto envy, strive ambitiously for positions of influence, and deem it the greatest happiness to be served, and to be exempt from the drudgery of servile tasks. The world itself does not dispute the difficulty of Christ-like virtue; it rather exaggerates its difficulty, and pronounces it utopian and impracticable – merely a beautiful, unattainable ideal (Bruce 1988, 352).

Yet, if there is to be a sensitive handing over of missions work by missionar-ies to indigenous leaders, both must show this virtue of humility that seeks to serve others even if it means coming down to the most menial service.

We also see how Jesus exemplified partnership when he called his disci-ples his friends. Notice that this was towards the end of his public ministry, having been with them for a period of about three years. During this period he had been teaching them about God and his way of salvation. He said to them, "No longer do I call you servants, for the servant does not know what his master is doing; but I have called you friends, for all that I have heard from my Father I have made known to you" (John 15:15). In other words, these men had matured under his instructions. They were ready to take up the task of leadership. He had taught them everything they needed to know. Henceforth, they were going to be treated as friends – as partners in the work.

Kostenberger notes:

> No longer does Jesus call the disciples servants; now he calls them friends. 'Friends' is a status more elevated even than 'disciples.' Whereas servants or slaves are simply told what to do, friends are given more information, which enables them to attain fuller understanding in their obedience . . . Yet the disciples' status as Jesus 'friends' is not an idle privilege; it carries with it a solemn responsibility and is granted in the context of being sent on a mission (Kostenberger 2004, 459).

Bruce also notes:

> The disciples had been apprentices, the apostles would be partners; the disciples had been government clerks, the apostles would be confidential ministers of the king; the disciples had been pupils in the school of Jesus, the apostles would be the treasurers of Christian truth, the reporters and expositors of their Master's doctrine, the sole reliable sources of information concerning the letter and spirit of his teaching. What office could possibly be more important than theirs? And how needful that they should realize their responsibilities in connection with it! (Bruce 1988, 422).

This is very important for missions work. A missionary goes into an area to evangelize. In due season, God gives him converts that he must work with and train into leaders. To begin with (in the first phase of the work), therefore, he instructs them from the top down (i.e. in a paternalistic way). But, according to the example of Christ, this must soon change into mutual partnership. The missionaries must deliberately work towards this. If the Lord Jesus, who is the Son of God and the fountain of knowledge itself, could do this to his disciples, then surely it should not be difficult for humans to do it to one another also? This will only happen when missionaries are humble enough to notice the fruit of their ministries in the people whom they have brought up. This fruit must make them admire the work of God in their lives.

Finally, Jesus could say, "I glorified you on earth, having accomplished the work that you gave me to do . . . I have manifested your name to the people whom you gave me out of the world . . . *Now they know* that everything that you have given me is from you. For I have given them the words that you gave me, and they have received them and *have come to know* in truth that I came from you; and they have believed that you sent me . . . As you sent me into the world, so I have sent them into the world." (John 17:4–8, 18, emphasis added).

It is instructive to note that Jesus said this before he went to the cross. The work that he had finished did not include redemption yet. Rather, it was that of teaching the disciples so that they could carry on the work of establishing the kingdom of God on earth through the gospel after his departure. One of the most important assignments that Jesus had to accomplish was that of teaching his disciples. Now that had taught them and nurtured them into leaders that could take over the work, he could say he had now finished his work on earth. He was ready to die and go to heaven. He had worked himself out of a job. It is this sensitive handover process that the researcher is seeking to emulate in this thesis.

The disciples were very reluctant to let the Lord Jesus Christ go. D. J. Pentecost took particular note of Peter's effort to stop Jesus going forward with his plans to die. He wrote:

> Peter vigorously sought to prevent Christ from going to Jerusalem where death would certainly ensue. There can be no question that Peter, conscious of the authority that had been conferred on him, felt responsible to prevent what seemed to be a catastrophe. Peter evidently was willing to use physical restraint if necessary on Christ (Pentecost 1981, 253).

The disciples had been used to having Jesus around and referring all queries to him. However, Jesus knew that unless he withdrew, they would never really become independent of him. Hence, he kept assuring them that he was going to provide for them in his absence by sending his Holy Spirit to be with them. However, his going was non-negotiable. Jesus said to his disciples:

> I will ask the Father, and he will give you another Helper, to be with you forever, even the Spirit of truth, whom the world cannot receive, because it neither sees him nor knows him. You know him, for he dwells with you and will be in you. I will not leave you as orphans; I will come to you. Yet a little while and the world will see me no more, but you will see me. Because I live, you also will live. In that day you will know that I am in my Father, and you in me, and I in you (John 14:16–20).

Often, once missionaries have established an indigenous leadership, the new leader will be very reluctant to see them withdraw because they feel a sense of safety with the missionaries around. However, they must withdraw from them – even if it is not in terms of a complete departure. They need to learn to exist and work without using the missionaries as crutches. That is what Jesus did here.

Jesus ended his earthly ministry by giving to his trained disciples what has come to be known as the Great Commission. He said, "All authority in heaven and on earth has been given to me. Go therefore and make disciples of all nations, baptizing them in the name of the Father and of the Son and of the Holy Spirit, teaching them to observe all that I have commanded you. And behold, I am with you always, to the end of the age" (Matt 28:18–20).

Speaking about the example that Jesus left for us here, Abendroth wrote:

> Pastors and New Testament leaders must reproduce themselves, while congregations need to be ready to be stretched and taught through discipleship. The Gospel of Matthew

ends with what is commonly (and rightly) called the 'Great Commission'. Christ's last words before his ascension contain the marching orders for his disciples and for every disciple of Christ throughout history. He is going to leave the disciples soon, and the timing of these words gives them greater significance and emphasis, or gravitas (Abendroth 2008, 97).

With that, the handover process was done and Jesus returned to heaven.

3.4 The Example of the Apostles

What about the apostles of our Lord Jesus Christ? How did they work themselves out of their jobs? When it came to the time for them to also raise the next generation of leaders; what was their attitude towards them? As with the example of Christ, we will analyse the biblical data by going through the three phases of church planting missions work and see how the apostles went about each of these phases. The researcher posits that the spirit of mutual respect and admiration will soon be evident, especially in the last phase of the work.

3.4.1 The initial paternalistic phase

As with the Lord Jesus Christ, whenever they entered a new sphere of ministry, there was an inevitable paternalistic phase. They had the truths, while the people to whom they came were living in ignorance. Hence, they spent the first phase of their ministry evangelizing and teaching the whole populace (Acts 13:16, 16:13–14, 17:1–2, 17:22, etc). Then, as they won disciples to Christ, they would proceed to teach them while continuing in their evangelistic work (Acts 13:43, 15:35, 17:4, etc). Since this is not the chief sphere of argument for this thesis, the researcher will not spend any more time seeking evidence for this in the Bible.

3.4.2 The shared leadership phase

Then came the stage where the disciples they had won to the Christian faith had matured to the point where they could appoint leaders among them. It was evident at this stage that they entered into the phase of a shared leadership.

The first challenge at this stage is the choice of leaders. When this researcher looked at the qualifications that the apostle Paul urged upon Timothy and Titus for the office of elder, he was struck that none of them had anything to do with a person's social standing in society – perhaps based upon his huge bank account. There was nothing there about how a person appeared on the outside. There was nothing there about the level of a person's secular education. All the qualifications in 1 Timothy 3 and Titus 1 are moral and spiritual qualifications.

> An overseer must be above reproach, the husband of one wife, sober-minded, self-controlled, respectable, hospitable, able to teach, not a drunkard, not violent but gentle, not quarrelsome, not a lover of money. He must manage his own household well, with all dignity keeping his children submissive, for if someone does not know how to manage his own household, how will he care for God's church? He must not be a recent convert, or he may become puffed up with conceit and fall into the condemnation of the devil. Moreover, he must be well thought of by outsiders, so that he may not fall into disgrace, into a snare of the devil (1 Tim 3:2–7).

> This is why I left you in Crete, so that you might put what remained into order, and appoint elders in every town as I directed you – if anyone is above reproach, the husband of one wife, and his children are believers and not open to the charge of debauchery or insubordination. For an overseer, as God's steward, must be above reproach. He must not be arrogant or quick-tempered or a drunkard or violent or greedy for gain, but hospitable, a lover of good, self-controlled, upright, holy, and disciplined. He must hold firm to the trustworthy word as taught, so that he may be able to give instruction in sound doctrine and also to rebuke those who contradict it (Titus 1:5–9).

The list of qualifications that we read in these two letters of the apostle Paul should challenge us to look primarily for spiritual maturity. As we shall see later, if Olive Doke and her fellow missionaries had used social standing as part of the qualifications for leadership, Paul Kasonga – who was a leper – would have never made it. Thankfully, like the apostles in the New Testament, they based their choice on the person's inner spiritual maturity. Once we learn to look for qualifications at such a level, we will find ourselves in relationships of mutual respect and admiration with people who are of a lower social standing than ourselves because we do not emphasize such outward matters.

The next task after choosing leaders is to work with them in true partnership. This is for the purpose of developing them into the kind of leaders that can truly run the church. As Dr J. Allen (2008, 56) says, "Church plants are not technological products cranked out from assembly lines; they are spiritual and living organisms. We are in the business of spiritually developing people."

The apostles did everything they could to remove any sense of paternalism as they entered into this stage of their work. In the book of Acts we see that the apostles did their church-planting work in teams. Many of those who were in the teams were not themselves apostles, but they still treated them as equals. For instance, notice how Luke records the way in which Paul's team was guided to go to Philippi.

> So, passing by Mysia, they went down to Troas. And a vision appeared to Paul in the night: a man of Macedonia was standing there, urging him and saying, "Come over to Macedonia and help us." And when Paul had seen the vision, immediately we sought to go on into Macedonia, concluding that God had called us to preach the gospel to them (Acts 16:8–10, ESV).

Notice the final inclusiveness! Whereas it was Paul who saw the vision, he brought it to the whole team to decipher what God's message to them collectively was. Hence, Luke's narrative changes at that point from the third person singular to the first person plural. This sense of ownership and responsibility only occurs where mutual respect is evident between all the team members.

John Stott refers to the importance of this in order for us to discern the Lord's mind for the future of our work in missions. He writes, "From this we may learn that usually God's guidance is . . . also corporate (a sharing of the data with others, so that we can mull over them together and reach a common mind)" (Stott 1990, 261). Where there is genuine partnership, without paternalism on one hand or an inferiority complex on the other, you will have the benefit of the multitude of counsellors. This is what the apostles sought to inculcate in the minds of their team members in this shared leadership.

The *Baptist Mission of Zambia Policy* document captures something of this when it says,

> Like Jesus, Paul carefully chose potential leaders and concentrated his efforts upon them. At various times and places, we find Paul working with leaders like Timothy, Aquila and Priscilla, Philemon and others. In 2 Timothy 2:2, Paul, in writing to Timothy emphasized, "And the things that thou hast heard of me among many witnesses the same commit thou to faithful men who shall be able to teach others also." Paul's answer to the problem of world evangelization was not a matter of simple addition but the principle of multiplication through the creation of reproducing Christians. While great emphasis can be given to money and methods, men are God's means of producing responsible churches.

> So it must be today. We are engaged in the Lord's work, not ours, and like Paul, we are called upon to give assistance, realizing that effective growth depends ultimately on the power of God. In missions the answer is partnership, not paternalism (1984, 9).

This phase of shared leadership is only meaningful where the missionary is willing to work in complete transparency with the new leaders. As long as some aspects of the ministry are exclusively for the eyes and ears of the missionary, then the next phase of the final handover cannot happen. The apostles worked hard to reach this level of transparency with the new leaders of the churches.

An example of this transparency in partnership is found in the way the apostle Paul handled the benevolent gift from Macedonia to the churches in Judea. He worked with the churches and their leaders in a very transparent way. He wrote:

> But thanks be to God, who put into the heart of Titus the same earnest care I have for you. For he not only accepted our appeal, but being himself very earnest he is going to you of his own accord. With him we are sending the brother who is famous among all the churches for his preaching of the gospel. And not only that, but he has been appointed by the churches to travel with us as we carry out this act of grace that is being ministered by us, for the glory of the Lord himself and to show our good will. We take this course so that no one should blame us about this generous gift that is being administered by us, for we aim at what is honourable not only in the Lord's sight but also in the sight of man. And with them we are sending our brother whom we have often tested and found earnest in many matters, but who is now more earnest than ever because of his great confidence in you. As for Titus, he is my partner and fellow worker for your benefit. And as for our brothers, they are messengers of the churches, the glory of Christ (2 Cor 8:16–23).

This phase of shared leadership lasted almost permanently in the church in Jerusalem because that became like the headquarters of the church in general. Hence, most of the apostles remained there. Yet, even there, they functioned as equals with the elders of the church. A classic example of this mutual respect between the apostles and the new leaders (elders) in the churches is found in Acts 15 when these two groups came together to resolve the difficulties threatening the peace of the church in Antioch. It is evident from the chapter that there was no superior attitude on the part of the apostles. They dealt with this matter as equals under the guidance of the Word of God and the Spirit of God. Luke wrote:

> But some men came down from Judea and were teaching the brothers, "Unless you are circumcised according to the custom of Moses, you cannot be saved." And after Paul and Barnabas had no small dissension and debate with them, Paul and Barnabas and some of the others were appointed to go up to Jerusalem to the apostles and the elders about this question. . . . The apostles and the elders were gathered together to consider this matter. . . . Then it seemed good to the apostles and the elders, with the whole church, to choose men from among them and send them to Antioch with Paul and Barnabas. They sent Judas called Barsabbas, and Silas, leading men among the brothers, with the following letter: "The brothers, both the apostles and the elders, to the brothers who are of the Gentiles in Antioch and Syria and Cilicia, greetings." (Acts 15:1-2, 6, 23 ESV).

One cannot miss the partnership in the leadership of the church between the missionaries – the apostles – and the new leaders of the church – the elders.

Gordon Keddie observes this fact in his commentary. He writes:

> The Jerusalem Council, as it has been named, was *a convocation of ordained elders* together with the apostles. The significance of this council, beyond the immediate decision which was made, lies in the fact that the apostles did not make the decision for the church, as could well have been expected of men of their unique position and gifts, but participated, for the purposes of this decision, as elders with the other elders, albeit as the "first among equals" (Keddie 1993, 173).

In other words, the apostles worked in partnership with the new leaders of the church without any air of extra authority. It was in an atmosphere of mutual respect.

3.4.3 The final withdrawal phase

Finally, the time came when they needed to move a few steps backwards and allow the indigenous leaders to lead the work. Even though they were apostles, they allowed this to happen so that local leadership would own the work without the apostles always peering over their shoulders.

One of the immediate areas in which the apostles took a few steps backwards was in the handling of the ordinances – the Lord's Supper and baptism. When it came to the conducting of the ordinances, the apostles not only shared this responsibility with the new leaders or with those who were part of their missions teams, but they allowed them to do most of that work. This worked in Paul's favour when there were personality factions in the church in Corinth, with some claiming to be his followers. Paul could look back and see that he had hardly baptized any of the converts himself, despite the fact that he was involved in the founding of the church in Corinth. He wrote, "I thank God that I baptized none of you except Crispus and Gaius, so that no one may say that you were baptized in my name. (I did baptize also the household of Stephanas. Beyond that, I do not know whether I baptized anyone else)" (1 Cor 1:14–16, ESV).

Allen observes that:

> The elders appointed by St Paul had authority to ordain as well as to baptize. If then the first elders were appointed simply by St Paul they must be compared with the first converts who were baptized by St Paul. Just as he baptized three or four and then committed the responsibility for admitting others to those who he had baptized; so he ordained three or four and committed the authority for ordaining others into their hands (1991, 100).

From the succeeding chapters it is evident that the resident leaders in Corinth were handling even the conducting of the Lord's Supper, and so he had to be called in to rectify a number of serious omissions on their part. He wrote:

> But in the following instructions I do not commend you, because when you come together it is not for the better but for the worse. For, in the first place, when you come together as a church, I hear that there are divisions among you. And I believe it in part, for there must be factions among you in order that those who are genuine among you may be recognized. When you come together, it is not the Lord's Supper that you eat. For in eating, each one goes ahead with his own meal. One goes hungry, another gets drunk. . . . So then, my brothers, when you come together to eat, wait for one another – if anyone is hungry, let him eat at home – so that when you come together it will not be for judgment. About the other things I will give directions when I come (1 Cor 11:17–21, 33–34, ESV).

It is most likely that 1 Corinthians was written before elders were appointed in the church in Corinth. The church was very much in its infancy. Yet, the apostle Paul still allowed the leaders who were there to conduct baptisms and the Lord's Supper. It was all part of the effort to phase out so that the indigenous leaders would be able to do all the work themselves.

When one looks at the attitude that the apostles had in relating to the new leaders that were appointed over the churches they planted, there is a stark contrast with the patronizing attitude that we have just seen being addressed in the previous chapter. The apostles respected and admired the individuals whom they appointed into leadership. For instance, the apostle Peter writing to the elders of the various new churches, said:

> So I exhort the elders among you, as a fellow elder and a witness of the sufferings of Christ, as well as a partaker in the glory that is going to be revealed: shepherd the flock of God that is among you, exercising oversight, not under compulsion, but willingly, as God would have you; not for shameful gain, but

eagerly; not domineering over those in your charge, but being examples to the flock. And when the chief Shepherd appears, you will receive the unfading crown of glory (1 Pet 5:1–4, ESV).

The apostle Peter addressed himself merely as "a fellow elder and a witness of the sufferings of Christ". There was no air of superiority about him. He was their partner in the work and he preferred to leave it that way. Thus the efficacy of his appeal lay more in its reasonableness than in the extraordinary nature of his office in the church as an apostle.

The admiration of the apostles for the men and women they were working with is observable in the way in which the apostle Paul often boasted about the men whom he appointed as leaders in the churches or who were in his leadership team. For instance, he wrote:

Now I urge you, brothers – you know that the household of Stephanas were the first converts in Achaia, and that they have devoted themselves to the service of the saints – be subject to such as these, and to every fellow worker and labourer. I rejoice at the coming of Stephanas and Fortunatus and Achaicus, because they have made up for your absence, for they refreshed my spirit as well as yours. Give recognition to such men (1 Cor 16:15–18).

As for Titus, he is my partner and fellow worker for your benefit (2 Cor 8:23)

I hope in the Lord Jesus to send Timothy to you soon, so that I too may be cheered by news of you. For I have no one like him, who will be genuinely concerned for your welfare. For they all seek their own interests, not those of Jesus Christ. But you know Timothy's proven worth, how as a son with a father he has served with me in the gospel (Phil 2:19–22).

It is evident from all this that the apostle Paul respected and admired them.

It is interesting to observe, too, that in the example that was referred to under the shared leadership phase, the apostles Paul and Barnabas allowed themselves to be sent back to Jerusalem to settle a doctrinal matter in a church that they themselves had planted. Why did Paul and Barnabas, who were apostles, allow this matter to be judged by fellow apostles and elders? It was not because they doubted their position. Rather, it was for the furtherance of the gospel, which can only take place in the context of unity. Curtis Vaughan puts it this way:

> Paul's intention in consulting with the Jerusalem apostles was not, we may be sure, to ascertain whether he and Barnabas were right or wrong in their proclamation of salvation for the Gentiles by the 'door of faith.' . . . Their concern was rather to silence the Judaizers, effect a proper understanding among the brethren, and work for unity in the church. The fear of the missionaries was that the opposition of the Jerusalem church – especially opposition of the leaders in that church – might render ineffectual both their past and future work among the Gentiles (Vaughan 1974, 98–99).

Yet, this is what has often happened where humility and true partnership has not been observed. The future usefulness of the missionaries has been curtailed.

It is interesting to note that when Luke referred to the leadership of the church in Antioch, after the labours of the apostles Barnabas and Saul (i.e. Paul), there was no sense of tier between the missionaries and the new leaders. He wrote, "Now there were in the church at Antioch prophets and teachers, Barnabas, Simeon who was called Niger, Lucius of Cyrene, Manaen a member of the court of Herod the tetrarch, and Saul" (Acts 13:1). This must have been because they were simply working as a team, with no effort to divide along the lines of missionaries and indigenous leaders.

Also, it is equally interesting that when God spoke to them about the need for Barnabas and Saul to continue their church-planting work in other areas, that these two apostles subjected themselves to ordination by the new leaders! "While they were worshipping the Lord and fasting, the Holy

Spirit said, 'Set apart for me Barnabas and Saul for the work to which I have called them.' Then after fasting and praying they laid their hands on them and sent them off" (Acts 13:2–3). It is this recognition that the leaders that have been set in place can even set apart the missionaries – even if they were apostles – for their new phase of ministry that shows that the final stage has been reached.

H. I. Hester captured this moment very well when he stated that,

> Under the ministry of Barnabas and Saul the church came to realize its obligation to take the gospel to other people. This strong church was to have the honour of serving as a centre from which three great campaigns for the proclaiming of the gospel to gentile people were launched (Hester 1981, 267).

Barnabas and Saul were not willing to make any false sense of self-importance take away from the importance of this next stage of the work. Thus they subjected themselves to be set apart for this next stage of work by the leaders in Antioch.

Even when their work was done, Saul (now Paul) and Barnabas returned to the very church they had planted and to the very leaders they had earlier ordained in order to render an account to them for the work they had done. Luke records, "From there they sailed to Antioch, where they had been commended to the grace of God for the work that they had fulfilled. And when they arrived and gathered the church together, they declared all that God had done with them, and how he had opened a door of faith to the Gentiles. And they remained no little time with the disciples" (Acts 14:26–28). This sense of accountability to fellow leaders, even if we are the ones who initially set them apart for the work, goes a long way to show that we have worked ourselves out of a job. The final phase was truly accomplished.

In the light of this, it is worth noting that the apostle Paul was very reluctant, where a leadership was already in place, to use his authority as an apostle to get things done. He preferred to teach rather than command. He preferred to persuade by force of argument, rather than simply demand blind obedience. By this conscious effort, he sought to develop the churches into self-governing entities. They went forward according to the light of knowledge they had, rather than always peeping over their shoulders wondering what the apostle Paul may think about their actions.

The *Baptist Mission of Zambia Policy* document states:

> Paul came as a minister to lead men to Christ, who is life. He did not introduce any practice to be received on his own human authority. He tried to make the converts realize and understand his relationship to Christ. He tried to convince minds, to stir consciences. He did not win obedience by decree, but through approval and cooperation. Paul did not do everything for the converts, but instead he let them do things for themselves. He set the example of Christ in his life, and the Spirit persuaded the people and they adopted the same for their own.
>
> We also see that Paul removed himself from the forefront, not through force but willingly. He gave the first place to Christ. He was always happy when converts progressed without him. He welcomed their liberty (McNeely 1984, 7–8).

Finally, the apostle Paul (as with the Lord Jesus Christ and all the other apostles) would consider his work done once the handover process was done. Hence, Paul could write to the Romans, saying, "But now, since I no longer have any room for work in these regions, and since I have longed for many years to come to you, I hope to see you in passing as I go to Spain" (Rom 15:24). That statement did not mean that all the people were now totally evangelized and discipled, but rather that he had finished the handover process of the work to indigenous leaders. His work was done. He had worked himself out of a job. He was now ready to move on to yet another sphere of work. It is this sensitive handover process that we are seeking to emulate in this thesis.

As with the Lord Jesus Christ, there was reluctance from the church leaders when time came for Paul to leave (Acts 20:36–21:1). However, again like the Lord Jesus Christ, Paul insisted that he needed to leave and literally tore himself away from the leaders of the church at Ephesus to whom he delivered his farewell address. H. I. Marshall captures something of this moment when he writes:

> Paul's consciousness that he would not return to Asia led him to take a last opportunity of speaking to the church leaders before he set off for Jerusalem with the probability of arrest and imprisonment there. . . . In the first section, verses 18–27, Paul looks back over his own work as a missionary. He describes how he had performed his work faithfully . . . He emphasizes that he has taught them fully and that the responsibility for what they have heard now rests in their own hands. These thoughts lead into the second section, verses 28–35, in which Paul instructs the church leaders for the future when he will no longer be with them. They are to follow in his example of faithful service . . . (Marshall 1984, 328–329).

3.5 Conclusion

From the above analysis it is evident that in the pioneering stage of the Christian faith, the work went through a number of phases, which ensured a sensitive handover from the 'missionaries' to the 'indigenous leaders'. Although the first phase was invariably paternalistic, as soon as the first leaders were appointed, there seems to be some evidence of progression and change from paternalism to true partnership. This progression is apparent in both the Lord Jesus and the apostles. The Lord Jesus said that he was no longer calling his disciples servants, but friends, because he had now taught them everything that they needed to know in order for them to take the work forward. The apostles started referring to themselves as "your fellow elders" because they had appointed elders in the churches and were willing to work with them as equals.

Also, there seems to be progress towards an exit in both the Lord Jesus Christ and the apostles as they near the end of their ministries. They provided sufficient training during the shared leadership stage to ensure that when they were gone, the work would continue to grow under the leadership of the new leaders. As for the apostles, they were even willing to become accountable to the new church leaders that they themselves had set in place. They finally handed over the work to individuals whom they both respected and admired.

In this thesis, we wish to see in a more recent example how Olive Doke and Paul Kasonga related to each other in a spirit of mutual respect and admiration for this to happen. Then, together with this biblical interpretation of missions, we hope to see how we can learn from this in order to ensure a sensitive and seamless handover process as we engage in church planting missions today.

CHAPTER 4

The Lives of Olive Doke and Paul Kasonga

4.1 Introduction

This chapter is the core of this research. It consists the sum of the gleanings from the tit-bits of the respective lives of these two servants of the Lord. Tracing their lives from childhood to how they separately found themselves at the same mission station, the researcher will go on to show how they worked together and progressively leadership of the church at the mission station was handed over to Paul Kasonga by Olive Doke. The biographical sketch will end with a summary, as an epilogue, of the life of Olive Doke after Kasonga's death. The chapter will end with a few concluding observations concerning the interest of this thesis in these two lives.

4.2 The background of Olive Doke

Titus Presler has observed that, "The rooting of Christianity in Africa takes place in a complex of historical backgrounds. These include African cultures, religions and political structures, mission work by both European and African agents, and the legacy of colonialism. Mission history finds its relevance in the fact that many African churches have been shaped substantially by missionaries in their liturgies, moral codes, theologies and institutional structures" (Presler 1989, 162). This is the context in which Olive

Doke and Paul Kasonga laboured at the pioneer stage of Baptist work in Northern Rhodesia (which is now called Zambia).

We come now to a consideration of the lives of Olive Doke and Paul Kasonga to see how the two exemplify the sensitive handing over process of missions work from the missionary to the indigenous leadership. As I have already stated, this is a piece of history that deserves a place among the most well known biographies in the realm of missions. Its neglect for over fifty years is unjustifiable.

For the purpose of this thesis, I will combine the story of these two lives. Although Paul Kasonga was the first to arrive at Kafulafuta Mission in Northern Rhodesia, beating Olive Doke by a few months, I will use the life of Olive Doke as the main narrative into which I will weave that of Paul Kasonga. This is for two main reasons:

1. Olive Doke was the international missionary who was to sensitively handle the handover process of missions to an indigenous leader. Hence, making her life-story the chief narrative only makes sense if we are to appreciate how this handover was done.

2. In terms of biographical material, I have much more information on Olive Doke than I have on Paul Kasonga. She was born earlier and lived much longer than he did. Also, she sent reports of her activities back to the South Africa Baptist Mission (SABM) and so scouring through these reports provides much more information for me into which I can weave the life of Paul Kasonga.

So, then, who was Olive Doke?

Olive Carey Doke was born in Bristol, England, on 26 September 1891. She was the second-born child and only daughter of the Reverend Joseph John Doke and Agnes Hannah Biggs. She had three brothers, William Henry, Clement Martyn and Vincent Comber. Part of her training in toughness must have come from growing up among three boys! She told a journalist later in life, "You see, I had to be a tomboy at an early age. So I had good training" (Jennings 1965, 15).

Born from grandparents who were involved in missions work, and from parents who were in the pastorate, Olive also grew up with the theme of evangelism and missions all around her. On her father's side she was related to William Knibb, a nineteenth-century missionary to Jamaica who championed the fight against slavery there. On her mother's side, she was also related to William Carey, the celebrated "founder of modern missions". Her middle name says it all! Her uncle, William Doke, became a missionary to Congo but died in 1883, a few years before she was born. Her father, Joseph J. Doke, really wanted to be a missionary, but was prevented from going into missionary service due to poor health, and so he became a Baptist minister. He started his pastoral ministry in England (Chudleigh and Bristol), and went on to pastor in New Zealand for a few years before finally settling in South Africa (Grahamstown and Johannesburg) in 1903 (Cursons 1929). Joseph Doke had a very strong desire to help the vulnerable and oppressed. While in New Zealand he fought for the cause of the Chinese who were marginalized in that country, and when he got to South Africa he joined hands with Mahatma Gandhi in fighting for the rights of Indians who were being discriminated against. This was the kind of home that Olive grew up in. Her father's passion must have rubbed off on her.

One interesting feature in the family of the Dokes when Olive was growing up was the friendship between her father, Joseph J. Doke, and the well-known Indian reformer, Mahatma Gandhi. In a country that was already separated along racial lines, this friendship taught Olive that someone's skin colour was not important. What mattered most was character. This was to help Olive a lot when she later met Africans like Paul Kasonga. Gandhi was particularly fond of the young Olive and maintained personal correspondence with her over many years, always addressing her as "My dear Olive". At least nine of those letters from 1908 to 1910 are still extant at the University of South Africa (UNISA) digital library. In one of them you can already sense the growing interest of Olive in girls' education, and literature, which became her passion when she became a missionary in Northern Rhodesia's Lambaland (Gandhi 1909).

In 1907, when Mahatma Gandhi was badly beaten up by his own people who were not impressed with his passive resistance approach in his historic reforms, he was taken to recuperate in the home of the Dokes. He wrote later, "Mr Doke and his good wife were anxious that I should be perfectly at rest. They therefore removed all persons from near my bed. I made a request that their daughter, Olive, who was then only a little girl, should sing for me my favourite English hymn, 'Lead Kindly Light'. Mr Doke liked this very much. He called Olive and asked her to sing in low tone. The whole scene passes before my eyes as I recall it. How shall I describe the service rendered me by the Doke family?" As we shall see later, she was to minister in this same way by the bedside of Paul Kasonga as he lay sick with leprosy.

About Olive's personal conversion to the evangelical Christian faith, little is known except that it took place during an evangelistic mission in New Zealand before she was even twelve years old. While on a trip to New Zealand in 1962, at the invitation of the Baptist Union there, she recollected this experience. She said:

> It was during my father's pastorate at Oxford Terrace that I gave my heart to the Lord at one of the Rev F. W. Boreham's missions, and even at that early age dedicated my life to missionary service. Shortly after this we went as a family back to England, where in 1903 my father had a 'call' to the Grahamstown Church in South Africa and later to the Central Church in Johannesburg. (Doke 1963, 4)

In terms of personality, those who knew Olive Doke as she grew up and even when she was serving the Lord in Lambaland, say that she was softspoken, shy and withdrawn, always keeping herself busy with something. Carina Bellin, who was to labour with Olive in the mission field for at least thirty-two years, said that Olive expressed herself more and better in writing. She wrote, "I doubt whether anyone who had not corresponded with Olive ever really knew her. She revealed herself in her letters far more than she did in personal contact. Writing was one of her many gifts" (Bellin 1973, 4).

4.3 Doke's And Kasonga's Early Labours

How did Olive finally find herself in Northern Rhodesia as a missionary? In 1913, her father and her brother, Joseph and Clement Doke, came to

Northern Rhodesia on a fact-finding mission soon after they heard that the first two Baptist missionaries in this part of the world (Henry Masters and William Phillips) were, due to financial problems, about to surrender the mission station in Lambaland.

Masters and Phillips had come from England and settled in the Kafulafuta area in order to bring the Baptist faith to Northern Rhodesia. After the death of David Livingstone in 1873, about fourteen Protestant mission societies had come into Northern Rhodesia, but Lambaland had not yet been taken up by any of them partly because of its sparse population. Lambaland covered about 30,000 square miles. Most of it was in Northern Rhodesia with a small portion of 6,000 square miles being in the Congo. In those days the population density was very low, about 3–4 persons per square mile. Ndola was the closest train station to Kafulafuta. Upon arrival there, you had to walk some forty miles to get to the mission station. After the visit by the Dokes, Joseph Doke died on his way back to South Africa. Clement Doke returned to Northern Rhodesia as the first South African missionary to this part of the world. Whenever his father had talked about his dreams for missions he talked about his boys going out to serve God in missions. Little did he know that his only daughter would go as well, and that she would outlast all her brothers in the mission field!

"In February 1915, Olive Doke, daughter of Joseph, applied for appointment as a missionary for Kafulafuta with most of her support to be contributed by her mother. She arrived in Kafulafuta in July 1916" (Saunders 1973, 52). Olive came to join her brother, Clement, as a missionary. He had already been in Kafulafuta for 2 years. She was only twenty-five years old when she arrived in Kafulafuta. For a girl of that age to leave the city life in well-developed Johannesburg and choose to live in the mud huts of the central African forest was something! Altogether at that time there were six missionaries working together in Kafulafuta. In the whole of the wider Ndola area, there were only two white women. She was the third! As for the wider Kafulafuta area, she was the first white woman most villagers would have ever seen (Jennings 1965, 13). When she arrived, the foundations for the Kafulafuta Baptist Church building were being built – the opening of the church building only took place a few months later in

December. Also the first printing of *Lambaland*, the mission quarterly sent to British supporters took place that same year. Olive later ran the mission's own printing press.

When Olive left Johannesburg, she was in the company of five other young ladies who were going out into the mission field in Northern Rhodesia. The others, who were in the company of Dr Walter Fisher, were going to Kalene Hill in the north-western part of Northern Rhodesia. Being with Dr Fisher gave her a great sense of assurance that she was in good hands because he was a veteran missionary in Northern Rhodesia. They had a stopover in Bulawayo to replenish their food supplies. Then, upon reaching Northern Rhodesia, they were all excited to see the famous Victoria Falls, with its water spray reaching into the sky. By the time the train crossed into Northern Rhodesia they were literally wet from the spray. They stopped over in Livingstone, which at that time was the capital of Northern Rhodesia. She described it thus; "Here was the customs place and the seat of government, but for all that, there was only one street lined with huge shady trees, two or three trading stores, post office, hotel and small hospital" (Doke 1964, 2). When they passed Lusaka, she commented that it was "only a siding for farmers in the district to be able to bring their produce to the line of rail". Doke finally reached Ndola around 04:00 hours.

Olive went through a serious cultural shock as she went to the mission field. She was particularly struck by the half-naked Africans all around, and often referred to this in her writing. Recalling her arrival on the mission field, Doke wrote"

> The train journey from Johannesburg to the siding of Ndola took five days and five nights (now it is two and a half days and three nights). Everything was leisurely – wood was burned in the engine after leaving Livingstone, the then capital, and this necessitated the firemen stopping the train and chopping a supply from time to time out of the forest and loading it aboard – that gave us time to stretch our legs! No such thing as a dining-car on that train – we had to have our own lunch baskets and when tea was required we took our tea-pot up to the engine for the boiling water! It was in the early hours of

the morning that the train came to a halt at Ndola siding, and I was dumped out with all my bags and baggage in the long grass. I had arrived in the area of my life's work! A group of half-naked Africans followed my brother, who had come in to meet me, and they all came to greet me, a little awestruck. These I learned were the carriers who had come to escort me out to Kafulafuta Mission, some forty miles away. This distance we had to travel on foot, making a camp on the way where the tents and stretchers were set up. My brother had brought the *machilla* (hammock carried by two men) and I was very glad to avail myself of it from time to time. (Doke 1966, 6)

One of the "half-naked Africans" referred to above was a boy of 14, who was to become her domestic servant for the next 42 years, until he died. His first duty was to prepare her first bath as soon as she arrived in Ndola. She then slept for a few hours before starting off for the forty-mile-long journey into the forest. They passed through Ndola town where Clement introduced her to its inhabitants – "the magistrate and his wife, two traders and their wives, and two bachelors running the A. L. C. Stores, who were also agents for the mission. That was the extent of Ndola in those days!" (Doke 1964, 4). Along the way, during that forty miles journey, they crossed and re-crossed the Kafulafuta River many times and crossed many plains and forests. Each village they reached they were greeted by the villagers who soon crowded around them and Clement preached to them. They stopped for the night in a village and Clement preached to the villagers. Doke described the scene; "The big fire showed up the naked bodies and gleaming eyes of the people as they gathered and seated themselves ready to listen to the message. It made a lump come into my throat to hear those people singing hymns to familiar tunes away there in the African forest. I longed to be used to bring many to a knowledge of salvation" (Doke 1964, 4). This was her first night in the forests of central Africa. She found it difficult to sleep. Long after everyone was asleep she was still awake, listening to the weird forest sounds of strange birds, lizards and wild animals. "Now, my new life had really begun," she thought to herself as she slowly fell asleep.

Doke describes their arrival at the mission:

> Towards late afternoon I noticed that the carriers had started
> singing vigorously again, a sign that we were nearing the mis-
> sion. Soon we could hear the school boys answering with their
> songs as they came out to meet us. Great was the excitement
> as we came face to face when rounding a huge anthill. The
> whole staff of Europeans was there and we all stood still as we
> gave thanks to God for his calling. There were over a hundred
> school boys and it was with difficulty that we could get along.
> They preceded us singing as they went and escorted us to the
> mission house. It was all bewildering and like a dream (Doke
> 1964, 7).

You would have thought that a twenty-five year old girl, leaving the bright
lights of Johannesburg, would be depressed by her new village home but
Doke's reaction was the exact opposite. She described her first home with
great joy:

> I was introduced to my room in the house shared with two
> other colleagues. A small long-shaped room, mud walls and
> mud floor with one grass mat on it, a camp-bed and chair.
> Another camp-table to serve as a dressing-table, and one for
> a wash-stand. There was also a very rough cupboard with
> shelves below and a bookcase above. No ceiling but just a
> slanting thatched roof and two windows in one wall. The win-
> dows opened like a fanlight and were gauzed for mosquitoes
> and wire-netted over outside for wild animals! It was indeed
> a 'prophet's chamber.' But, oh, how happy I was to be there
> where the Lord had called me and to realize that at last I was
> at Kafulafuta. My heart was full of praise and thanksgiving
> (Doke 1964, 8).

The next morning, her first day at the mission, she was given a guided tour around the mission station. She was shocked to see the terrible state of those who came to the mission for medical treatment. She wrote:

> It was not long after breakfast before the sick and maimed began to arrive for treatment, and I was horrified to see the terrible sores they were suffering from. Tropical ulcers which had eaten right down to the bone in some cases; toes swollen and suppurating with the jiggers worming their way into the flesh. It was all most revolting – but they had come for help. There were no modern drugs then. So a liberal use of permanganate and boracic powder and ointment was made, and it was amazing how things healed (Doke 1964, 8).

Mrs German, the other European woman in their mission house, was a semi-invalid and so Doke immediately took over most of the housekeeping duties. She also worked hard at developing an acquired taste for the local foodstuffs because that was what comprised most of their meals. She started a vegetable garden in order to add some English vegetables to the menu.

But what was the spiritual state of the Lamba people when Olive Doke arrived? These early missionaries found the Lamba people steeped in what they called "the unspeakable horrors of spirit worship, witchcraft, human sacrifice, live burials, and cannibalism". Thankfully, they found the Lamba people very docile and scattered because of fear of slave traders.

Perhaps this is the best place to introduce Paul Kasonga. Frey (2009, 68) writes, "It is nearly impossible to look at the history of the Baptist church in Zambia without mentioning the name Paul Kasonga. He had such a great influence among the Lamba people, that he cannot be forgotten." His original name was Kaputula (which means, short trousers) Kasonga. When Doke arrived at Kafulafuta Mission in July 1916, Kaputula had barely been there a few months. He would have been one of the school boys who came out to meet Doke when Clement brought her from Ndola.

Kaputula Kasonga was born about 1902. Very little, if anything, is known about him before he showed up at the doors of the mission school in Kafulafuta in order to pursue his education. This was towards the beginning of 1916, when he was about 14 years old. As he sat through the various Bible lessons, God soon opened his eyes to see his sinfulness and the all-sufficient salvation procured for him in the person and work of the Lord Jesus Christ. Thus one evening – on the 9th of July 1916 to be precise – he knocked on the door of one of the missionaries, Clement Doke, and asked if he could give his life to the Lord. "Shikulu Doke," he said, "I want to turn over my heart." Let us allow him to tell this event in his own words.

> I came to the Mission at Kafulafuta at the beginning of 1916 and in the middle of that year Walona Doke arrived. I was then a schoolboy and heard the Word of God from Shikulu Filipo and Shikulu Wale and Shikulu Doke. The words of a hymn we sang, "Jesus is coming again," arrested me and made me think, so I went to Shikulu Doke that night and had a talk with him and there and then gave my heart to the Lord (Doke 1955, 3).

That was the story of how one of the earliest converts among the Baptists in Zambia came to Christ – at about 14 years of age. When schools closed, Kaputula disappeared from school and did not return for the rest of that year. However, as the missionaries went around preaching the gospel from village to village they finally found him because of his witness. Each time they went to a village they would ask, "Have you heard of Jesus?" and the answer was invariably, "No, who is he?" But one day upon asking the same question in one village, they got the answer, "Yes, we have heard about Jesus. Kaputula told us about him." That is how they found their long lost convert. Sadly, they found that Kaputula had contracted leprosy and was segregated from the rest of the village. He was living alone across the river in a small hut. The missionaries organized for him to be brought to Kafulafuta and with the use of medicine were able to arrest the disease and Kaputula was able to continue his schooling.

Having learned how to read and write, Kaputula was assigned the task of accompanying Clement and Olive Doke to start a new school in Kawunda Chiwele. Kaputula recalled the event:

Shikulu Doke and Walona Doke went with me and Mose Katanga to open the school. They left us there while they went off itinerating in the villages. While there, Mose and I constantly preached the Word of God in the surrounding villages, and quite a number responded to the message and became Hearers. (Doke 1955, 4)

It was soon after this that Kaputula testified to the Lord's saving grace through the waters of baptism and changed his name from Kaputula to Paul. The day was 7 March 1920. Kaputula wrote:

> At that time we had only the Gospel of John and Mark, together with Jonah, in print in the Lamba language. These we read constantly. This reading and talks I had with Shikulu Filipo and Shikulu Doke led me to ask for baptism. I had never seen a baptism, but several of us were seeking baptism at the same time, so Shikulu Doke had classes for instruction with us. We were five: Katandika afterwards Luke Mavula and Ngolofwana being Reuben Chumpuka, and Chilayi his brother now known as Mako, and Jakobi Mununga and myself (Doke 1955, 5).

That is how Kaputula Kasonga became Paul Kasonga, named after the great apostle Paul.

Before we delve into the mutual labours of Olive Doke and Paul Kasonga, we need to have a feel of missions work in central Africa in those days. I will allow Doke to describe something of her experiences. Referring to those early years, Doke wrote:

> The work was still in the pioneer stages, and a great deal of 'trekking' had to be done, involving long journeys of hundreds of miles on foot through the African forest infested by wild animals of every description. It was still the days of primitive travel with native porters carrying the necessary camp equipment and barter goods. One had to depend on one's

rifle to secure meat for the pot, as well as to buy meal for the carriers. The country inhabited by the Lamba tribe extended over 30,000 square miles of forest – and this was our parish! (Doke 1963, 4)

Elsewhere, Doke reported:

> It took time to learn to walk long distances in the African bush on the narrow winding paths. There were no roads in this country nor even the wider hoed-open paths of later days. We were greeted by people as we passed through village after village of little mud huts with the spirit-huts quite prominent showing how ignorant they were of a loving Saviour and how much they needed to be taught. They were poor in every way, just subsisting on what they could grow in their gardens and forage from the forest. Each family had at least one hoe (hand-made) and an axe, also home-made, and they were very adept at using them. Everything they needed was either in the forest or in the rivers or on the plains. Poles for building their huts, bark-rope from the trees for tying the bamboo laths and grass from the plains for thatching the roofs – clay from the river banks for making their cooking pots – fish in the rivers and game to be trapped in the forest. What more would one want? Day after day the same routine – and they did not know that they sat in great darkness! One thing lacking – the light of the gospel! (Doke 1966, 6)

Pioneer missions work was hard work. Merely surviving in the forests of Africa demanded a lot! That is what Doke found when she came to Lambaland. They had to order their groceries from South Africa – nine months' worth at a time. This helped to reduce the monotony of their meals by adding tinned corned beef, salmon and sardines. Mail came in from Ndola once a week. As already described, they lived in huts with mud floors. To prevent termites eating their mats, these had to be rolled up each night. Also, the legs of the furniture had to be treated to save them from the same fate. There was no electricity and so they relied on candles and paraffin lamps for lighting at night. They were ever in danger of forest fires. Heat and rain were constant perils and droughts were fairly common. They hunted game in order for them to have meat to eat. Doke herself did quite a bit of hunting, especially when trekking through the forest on evangelistic trips or when she remained the only white missionary on the mission station, sometimes for years. She was licensed to carry a .303 sports rifle and a 12 bore double-barrelled shotgun. "When I got back from a trek of a few hundred miles it was nothing to go out for some thirty miles to shoot our dinner," she once told a reporter (Jennings 1965, 14). She claimed that she never learned to shoot: she just shot! Her first shot killed an antelope. "I don't know who was more surprised – the antelope or me." The largest snake she ever shot was a 12-foot long python. On one occasion while on a trek, when she ran out of quinine, she became very sick from malaria. Her carriers began to complain of hunger and so she asked them to carry her to the edge of a plain. She propped her rifle up on the shoulder of one of her carriers and aimed at a herd of antelope. She shot two antelopes with one bullet!

At that time the missionaries used hippo fat for cooking oil – they had no butter for many years. To avoid falling ill from malaria, they survived on a daily dose of quinine. It was never safe to be out at night because leopards, lions and hyenas were prowling around looking for food. In many cases they were the first white people to be ever seen by the villagers and so they caused quite some attraction! Travelling was extremely slow. The journey from Lusaka to Ndola, which takes just under four hours by car today, often took an entire week when done on foot in those days! They had an entire team of carriers with them and camped for the nights and preached the word of God in the villages along the way. This was the kind of life that Olive Doke lived when she came to Lambaland. Because Doke never got married, she never had to deal with the extra demands of pregnancy or running a home full of children or caring for a husband. Thus she was able to do much more than most married missionary wives would have done.

Like all other missionaries in those days, Doke had to learn the language of the people from the people themselves. Since Lamba was not yet a written language, she had to go out and live among the people so that she could hear them talking among themselves as they related to everyday situations. She would then try to share the Word of life with them in their own language. With time, she became more and more proficient and started to carry out translation work. This was a very difficult process both for the missionaries and the local people. Doke recollected the beginning of the learning process and said:

> Gradually in some of them who were in contact with us there awakened a desire to learn. It intrigued them that a few marks made on a bit of paper, and sent to a colleague, conveyed a message that was acted upon; and they wished to have this secret. They had no idea of all this would involve of concentration, hard work and stick-at-itiveness. It was interesting to see the awakening. And so they and we learned together. We had to learn their language and customs and set about translating the precious Word we had brought to them. There were long years of patient work before we had the privilege of giving them the whole Bible in their own language (Doke 1966, 6).

By 1921, Doke had successfully participated in the translation of the entire New Testament into Lamba, and participated in the writing of a Lamba grammar, a Lamba phrase book, and a collection of Lamba folklore and proverbs. She loved the Lamba language and often signed off her letters, even to none Lamba-speaking friends, with the words, "Mitende mwense, nine Walona Doke" (i.e. Lamba for "Greetings to all, I am Ms Doke").

Trekking and living in the heart of the forests of central Africa had its dangers, and many times Doke experienced the protecting hand of God. She testified of some of those occasions in blood-chilling detail.

> One occasion took place when we had settled ourselves in for the weekend near a group of villages. We found it was not such a good spot after all. After the services at night we went back to camp and chatted around the fire before turning in. It was not long after the camp was quiet that I heard in the distance a leopard calling and coming nearer and nearer. Then

I realized that they had cattle in stockades down by the village and that was the attraction. My carriers were sleeping outside, and my tent was without a stockade. We thought it was safe being so near to the village. The leopard came nearer, and then I heard another one answering it further back, but following the first one, then another and another joined in the concert until there were five distinct ones, and our camp was right in the path! I could hear the carriers stirring and on the alert, and knew that their spears were not far away. They passed close to us but did not turn aside, and later on I heard them again going off in the other direction. The protecting arm [of God] was around us.

The next night we were still in the same camp and towards evening I heard a terrific noise coming nearer and nearer. It sounded like a tornado, trees were crashing down and the ground began to shake. It was a herd of elephant on the rampage! Again, I hoped that we were not in their direct line, for the camp would have been flattened. Again the Lord protected us and they passed only a few hundred yards from us, tearing down the trees and trumpeting in their fury.

Many years later, I experienced the same loving protection from a very dangerous snake in my office. I was sitting at my desk busy with revision work on the New Testament when I heard a hissing sound subconsciously and did not take any notice, thinking it was the boy drawing water from the tank at the back. But it persisted and I thought I would go and see what it was. As I stood up a big black cobra fell from the bookcase behind me and landed at my feet and then disappeared into the other bookcase. I called loudly for my 'boy' to bring spears, and he came running. Cautiously we moved out the tables and chairs from the corner to clear the decks for action. One by one, we hooked out the packets of books at the bottom, when all of a sudden his head appeared over a packet on the next shelf above, fangs out and beady eyes looking at us. We made several thrusts with the spears before we pinned a part of his body to the wall – but that was not good enough. We had to get his head, which was most difficult as he was dodging behind the supports of the bookshelf. I held him down with one spear at arm's-length while James tried to get his head. He spat, and from that distance he got the spittle onto my glasses and into my mouth, but James escaped fortunately. The poison was horribly bitter, but I had the sense not to swallow and held on while he squirmed and hissed and fought. Eventually I pinned his head down against the wall and the brute wriggled his body up behind the next shelf. With him pinned down with the two spears I was holding, James had to pull all the books out to get at him. Slithering and sliding and writhing we dragged him outside on the point of a spear. He tried to get away and we had to bash his head to pulp. With him dispatched I went off to get some permangate to wash my mouth out, and then over to Miss Bellin to get a shot of penicillin. I am thankful that the spittle did not get in my eyes because that would mean blindness. There is something to say for wearing glasses! (Doke 1964, 23).

We have already noted the conversion of Kaputula Kasonga. But one of the first outstanding conversions that Doke witnessed on the mission field was that of a government messenger called Kasyonka. This took place in 1918. Kasyonka was a polygamist with two wives and was hated by the people because he was cruel and hard. All his children died in infancy. When the boys in his neighbourhood went home for holidays from the Kafulafuta boarding school, he heard from them about Jesus and so he went with a friend to the mission station to find out more about this Jesus. Day after day he returned to the mission to hear more. Often, as the story of redemption was recounted, tears would be seen rolling down his cheeks. Soon the Lord saved him and he became a changed man. He was baptized and given the name Inoki (Enoch). He quickly made peace with all his enemies. Many people could hardly believe what had happened to him. When he learned that marriage had to be monogamous, he tried to divorce his second wife but she threatened to commit suicide. So, in the end he lived with both his wives. They later became Christians and were also baptized. Their home became a wonderful example of godliness and Christian love.

The stories of the conversions of Kaputula and Kasyonka are just two examples of the many wonderful conversions that took place in these early years in Lambaland. The environment, however, made it very difficult for many of the converts to maintain their witness and so a lot of patience was required on the part of the missionaries. Doke also realized this. "As the time passed Miss Doke realized that a great deal of patience had to be exercised with the Lambas. They had such a history of superstition and witchcraft, that after accepting Christ, many would fall back time and time again before making a total surrender to the demands of the gospel. Once this stage was reached by the believer, he would become an active evangelist among the people" (Meier 1975, 57). This was soon to be true of a number of the early converts – including Kaputula, who was now Paul Kasonga.

The first assignment that Paul Kasonga had as a preacher was a call that came from Chirupula, some one hundred miles south-east of Kafulafuta. Chirupula was a nickname given to a white farmer, J. E. Stephenson, who lived in the area, because of his fierce whipping. He had become so much part of the life of the area that he had even married African wives and had children with them. This is the man who had asked the Mission Superintendent to send them a teacher who could open a school on his farm. The lot fell on Kasonga. How he responded to this call and how his ministry went there are best told in Kasonga's own words:

> At first I refused to go because I was afraid of the fierceness of Chirupula, but Shikulu Filipo talked with me and strength-ened me by reminding me of the story of Joseph when he was sold into Egypt. He said I must not be afraid for it was God who wanted me to witness and work for Him there. His words strengthened my heart and I consented to go. I went in faith that strength would be given me and that God would go before me, and He did. When I arrived I found that my fears were groundless, for Chirupula received me very kindly and trusted and liked me, and I was very pleased and happy. There, too, I used to go to the surrounding villages, when my

work was done, and give out the gospel message. I had charge of Chirupula's six children for the school hours. His two wives and the wife of the neighbouring doctor were very interested in the words I had to tell them about Jesus, and often came to talk with me . . .

On Sundays I gathered the people on the estate at Chiwefwe for a service, if I was not out in the villages . . . Bwana Chirupula was so pleased with me and with the fact that he could trust me that he did not want me to ever leave him. In fact, when I intimated that I wanted to go home and rest, he got angry and said he would report me to the Magistrate at Ndola. His brother Peter, though, told him that that was not right and that if I was happy I would come back after a rest. So the Bwana consented to my going home for a holiday and Reuben Chumpuka was sent down to take my place. By the time I got back to Kafulafuta I found that Shikulu Doke and his wife had left to go down South and that Shikulu Cross had come to take his place and Walona Stern had come to keep Walona Doke company. That was in 1921 (Doke 1955, 6).

Kasonga used to smoke as a Christian. He never smoked in the presence of the missionaries in Kafulafuta because they discouraged anyone from smoking. In fact, they punished the school boys if they found them smoking. But now that Kasonga was alone in Chirupula he smoked publicly, and yet it was while he was in Chirupula that he gave up the habit completely. How did that happen? In Chirupula there was a strong Seventh-Day Adventist presence and they taught that Christians did not smoke. So, when Kasonga went around the villages preaching the gospel, the people were confused to see him smoking also. As this apparent contradiction came to his attention, he was so convicted of it that he prayed to God to help him overcome this addiction and the Lord helped him. That was how he stopped smoking.

Kasonga's return to the mission was not really a holiday. He learned carpentry from the missionaries – a very useful skill in those days. He also soon got involved in preaching the gospel and many people came to the knowledge of the Saviour through his preaching.

Kasonga's holiday was soon over and he returned to Chirupula. However, his return was short-lived, as the leprosy had returned. He was taken back to his small village hut across the river from his village. The disease spread quickly and sores developed all over his body. He was such a pitiful sight. All kinds of herbal medicines were used to try and cure him, but it was all in vain. Kasonga trusted in his God and spent almost all his time reading the Lamba New Testament, which had only come into print that year. In due season, his fingers and his toes dropped off, and so his younger brother, who used to bring his food, would turn the pages for him as he read the Scriptures. God spoke to him through its pages and he grew in spirit by leaps and bounds. One day an African diviner came to offer to heal him, but Kasonga could not accept this. "If you will use your medicine without any of your witchcraft incantations and spirit worship, I will accept it; but if not – go!" The diviner was impressed by Kasonga's stance and offered to try and help without any of his spiritism and worship. He burned powerful medicinal herbs and applied them to Kasonga's body and that is how he slowly began to heal.

Kasonga wrote to Olive Doke and the other missionaries at Kafulafuta about his healing and asked if he could go and join them once again. They were surprised to hear from him because they had lost hope that they would ever see him again and they gladly consented to his return. They sent two men with a hammock to go and collect him. When they returned, the missionaries thought they came back with an empty hammock. Kasonga was in there but he had become so thin that he was just skin and bones. He could not even walk. Olive Doke and the other missionaries wept when they saw what the disease had done to him. As for Kasonga, he was still all smiles and full of joy at what the Lord had done for him. He was glad to be back among the brethren. With further medicine and good food, Kasonga was able to regain most of his strength and earlier body size. That was how Kasonga returned to Kafulafuta and he remained there for the rest of his life.

Having lost all his fingers and toes, Kasonga had to learn to walk and write again. As he regained his strength, he began to use a walking stick to walk around. In due season, he learned to walk on the stump that was left of his feet. Similarly, he learned to hold a pen in between the stump of his thumb that was left and his palm, and with practice learned to write again. As he developed in both walking and writing, he started taking some classes in the school again and was glad that he could be useful for the Lord once again.

4.4 Progress Despite Great Discouragements

The second quarter of the twentieth century saw tremendous changes in *Lambaland*. This began with the discovery of copper in the mid-1920s in what is now called the Copperbelt. New towns, with beautifully laid-out townships, began to spring up near the places where the copper was being mined. There was a great influx of European workers in the new and old towns. Africans also came in from different parts of the country to get jobs in these towns. Various industries providing all kinds of services to the mines also sprang up and thrived.

By the middle of the century there were excellent roads joining the major towns. Some of these roads were tarred while others were dirt roads, but wide and well maintained. However, with these developments also came all kinds of vices. Prostitution, alcohol abuse, and the breakdown of family life became more rampant. This new city life was having its own negative impact on life in the villages around Lambaland.

One individual who was terribly affected by this was one of the very first converts in Lambaland and the very first person baptized by the missionaries in 1910. His name was Sandabunga. He was the son of headman Katanga and soon became their first Lamba translator and local evangelist. So, Doke was filled with sorrow when on 22 April 1926, she stumbled across the fact that Sandabunga had taken a second wife despite his Christian knowledge. Doke talked with Sandabunga's first wife and discovered that this was no secret in the village, and that despite many appeals to him, Sandabunga had stubbornly insisted on keeping this new woman in his life. Doke prayed for wisdom and called Sandabunga the next day. She earnestly pleaded with him to get rid of this second woman, who in fact was also a Christian from another mission north of Kafulafuta. Thankfully, Sandabunga truly repented of his sin and took the woman to her brother in the mine township. Sandabunga made a public confession before the church and was restored.

The missionaries knew that their calling was that of evangelizing the people and so they pressed on with their work. The most difficult part was that of going from village to village, preaching the gospel. Yet, this work had to be done. The area they covered was from Broken Hill, Mkushi, Ndola, Kantanshi, and all the way into the Congo. Doke wrote in the Lambaland Magazine of 1923 something of their experience at this time as they went from village to village preaching the gospel: [[this is a block quote paragraph]]"The trying part of our journey began as we reached the swamps. I wish some of you folks could see the long grass through which we had to push our way, often without so much as a track to guide us. In some places we just had to burrow through it like rabbits – not knowing what we might meet in the semi-darkness of the tunnels that we made. At other times a path of sorts had been trodden down but the grass towered up on either side of us to a height of eight or twelve feet, quite shutting us in. Periodically, the path would open out into a great swamp through which we had to wade. In such surroundings as these, we would come across isolated villages, peopled by men and women for whom the Lord Jesus Christ had died, but who had so seldom heard His Name. I remember so well the day that we passed through six villages and slept at a seventh, and at none of them had His Name ever been heard, except once – from one of our evangelists. How one's heart yearns over them!"

That same year (1923) Doke acquired a bicycle for use on these long trips. Incidentally, she was the first person on the Copperbelt to own a bicycle!

On one of those treks Doke and her travelling companions got hopelessly lost in the forest. They asked for directions from a village but somehow took a wrong turn and kept going on until they came to an unknown village. Thankfully, as providence would have it, the story had a happily-ever-after ending. Many years later, Doke recalled this frowning providence and saw its happy ending. She said, "We found there a boy called Nikodemo Kapolobwe whom we took back to the mission for schooling. Later, it was this boy who opened up Baptist mission work in the western area of Nkana to Siwuchinga" (Jennings 1965, 15). After he died, the Nikodemo Memorial Church was built in the far west in his honour.

Doke's love for the indigenous people was evident to all as she travelled among the villages and ministered the Word of God to them. Hudson Litana, who was a young man in those days, but later became a pastor, said during an interview for this thesis, "Olive loved people. She taught the Word to people and liked teaching from the book of Hosea. She even once rebuked Clement [her brother] for segregation. She was very strong physically and used to walk on foot to preach the gospel. She was also very strong in the Lord" (Hudson 2010). Hudson later provided secretarial services for both Doke and Kasonga. His most recent appointment was that of secretary for the Lambaland Baptist Association. He is now in retirement.

Also speaking about Doke's love for the indigenous people, Isaac Lwambululwa recalled during an interview for this thesis, "Olive carried out her work like a man. She considered herself as one of the indigenous people. She was very caring and loving. She took care of us (my sister and I) like her own children and instructed us in the Word. She was a good teacher and would travel a lot."

Between 1920 and 1925, the missionaries were reduced to four – Phillips, Olive Doke, Arthur Cross and Frieda Stern, whom Cross married in 1923. Clement, who had earlier in 1919 married Miss Hilda Lehmann, had to leave in 1921 due to his wife's poor health. Phillips also resigned due to poor health in 1926. Since Arthur Cross and Frieda Stern found Olive Doke already on the mission field, by 1926 Doke had become the longest-serving foreign missionary at Kafulafuta. In fact, for several years after 1926, Doke was the only missionary remaining at Kafulafuta Mission. It was during this period that she also travelled the longest distance in one week. This took place in 1925 when the Prince of Wales was visiting Northern Rhodesia. Doke, being a Briton by birth, was keen to see him. So, she walked 110 miles from Kafulafuta to Broken Hill to see him and the journey took one week. One reason for the slowness of the journey was simply the fact that she was sharing the gospel from village to village as she made her way to Broken Hill.

Doke had a strong passion for the education of the girls. This was, in part, for spiritual reasons, because in the first few years of the work at Kafulafuta the converts were all males. It took many years before they had their first female convert. Olive noted that this was a real bottleneck in the advance of Christianity in Lambaland. Ira David Meier notes, "The women, Miss Doke realized, were in many cases holding their Christian husbands back in their faith, and began emphasizing her work among them. She maintained, and later proved to be correct, that unless Lamba women were won for Christ, little progress would be made" (1975, 57). So in the mid-1920s, she opened a boarding school for girls. However, this experiment came to a temporary halt after all twenty-five students ran off to become temporary wives at Luanshya's new Roan Antelope mine. Doke never gave up but soldiered on. The girls' school finally became well established and produced some of the first female leaders and teachers in the church in Lambaland. By 1965, forty years later, this school had about two hundred girls, with ninety-eight of them boarding.

> Originally, Miss Doke records that the children would use the ground to write on; each wiping the dust of the hard baked ground and scratching letters and numbers. The school day would consist of periods of Scripture instruction and also lessons of regular schoolwork. Each student would also be required to do several hours' work on the mission ground. This would mean digging in the gardens, brickmaking, thatch cutting, or any one of the numerous jobs to be done around a station. Before effective schoolwork could be achieved, the children, of a widely varying age, would have to learn to read. Being a pioneer work, Miss Doke wrote her own primer, called *Kace-Kace*, which was used in the school for many years. As the pupils progressed, Miss Doke found herself writing more and more reading instruction books. The ability to read was treasured among the Lambas and classes for older people were begun. In one instance, Miss Doke found that one woman who had learned to read took *Kace-Kace* home to her village and on passing through the village one day she found that the

woman had taught others in the village how to read. In the school, Miss Doke was able to give continual and sound biblical teaching and it was her privilege to see, years later, many of her ex-pupils standing for Christ and also serving in positions of leadership. There were no other teachers save the missionaries themselves when the mission started (Meier 1975, 69).

Right through the 1920s, the SABMS was having very serious financial difficulties and literally every year they were threatening to hand over the Kafulafuta mission to another missionary organization or just close it down completely. It was, therefore, solely because of the resoluteness of Doke and the Crosses that the work continued. It was during this time that yet another disaster befell Doke. Her mother used to come all the way from South Africa to visit her and work alongside her in Kafulafuta. However, on one of these trips, on her way back to South Africa, she died on 29 August 1929. Thus a major source of financial support and encouragement in Doke's life was no more.

In 1933, Doke had the unequalled joy of witnessing the baptism of an old lady who had been very special to her since she came to Kafulafuta. Her name was Chalwe. She was the sister to old chief Katanga and was greatly respected among the people. Doke always remembered the special welcome that this old lady gave her when she arrived at the mission for the very first time in July 1916. With a beaming smile on her old face, she gripped Doke's hand with a double handshake. From that time on, Chalwe was always the first to come out and welcome Doke to the mission, whenever she came from any evangelistic trip. They developed a very warm relationship and Doke shared the gospel with Chalwe many times. Illness and old age soon made Chalwe totally blind, and so she went about her business led by one of her grandchildren. One day, in 1931, Doke passed by her dilapidated home and found Chalwe in a pitiable state of illness with no one to look after her. She organized for this old lady to move in with her at the mission and she nursed her back to health. They spent many evenings together, as Chalwe told Doke many stories from early Lamba history. She was ever grateful for the day that the mission came to Kafulafuta.

It was during this period that Chalwe professed faith. Recounting the whole episode in the *Lambaland* of April 1934, Doke wrote:

> You may imagine that my heart gave a leap of thankfulness as I realized that at last our prayers on her behalf were being graciously answered. After talking and praying with her, I sent her down to Paul, for he makes things so very real to them . . . . Paul and I had long talked with her and pointed out what a real Christian should be like in the everyday life, wholly given up to God's will and guidance . . . We had a long talk together, Paul pleading with her to give up everything for Christ, who did so much for her and at last with a happy glow on her old lined face she said, "I will . . ." She attended the baptismal classes that Paul had so that she might fully understand the steps she was taking, and on the last Sunday of the old year [1933], she confessed her Lord in the waters of baptism (Doke 1934a, 3).

That was how Chalwe was baptized, being welcomed into church membership by Paul Kasonga. She remained a faithful member of the church until old age totally incapacitated her. She went to be with the Lord towards the end of 1938, full of years and full of faith. It was in the same year (1933) that Doke got a note from Paul Kasonga, which I will refer to later, telling her of the conversion of Chief Kacheya, whom they had been praying for with respect to his salvation. So, this was a year of glory in the midst of Doke's many woes.

Now back to Paul Kasonga. It was not long after Kasonga's return to Kafulafuta after his last ministry at Chirupula's homestead before he became the acknowledged African leader of the Lord's work among the Baptists not only at Kafulafuta, but in the whole of Lambaland. He was a born leader. His life was a wonder to behold. Even the missionaries noticed that they had a leader in their midst and so gave Kasonga the task of preaching in the morning services at the mission station. In 1931 for the first time the missionary reports going back to the South African Baptist Missionary Society included one African on the list of its leaders, and his name was Paul Kasonga. The people heard him gladly because he had a way with words in his mother tongue. No missionary could preach in Lamba as he did. Also, because he knew the mindset of his own people, he used the sword of the Spirit to drive out sin from the darkest recesses of their souls in a way that no missionaries could. He used a lot of illustrations in his preaching. His stories made biblical truths come alive. One moment he would have the worshippers roaring in laughter as they saw the folly of thoughts and customs, and the next moment he would use the same illustration to drive home very solemn truths with powerful conviction. Kasonga was also very involved in translation work. Because he knew the various shades of meaning behind the Lamba words, he was able to assist Doke and the missionaries find the right words as they translated various biblical texts and other books from English to Lamba. In fact, Peter Landani, born 1936, (in an interview for this thesis) says that Kasonga was very involved in the writing of *Kace-Kace*, the educational books mentioned earlier (Landani 2010). The full name of the series of books was *Kache Kache Kishimikisha Ifyamano*.

Writing in *Lambaland* in January 1931, Doke acknowledged her dependence upon Paul Kasonga, stating:

> Paul, as you know, is invaluable in this work; it is who he is in touch with them all, and it is on him I rely. While I have been away he has been able to make several trips, teaching and helping the people, advising them in their difficulties, staying with them for days at a time (Doke 1931a, 2).

Later in the same year, when Kasonga was taken ill, she again wrote:

> Now today Paul has been taken suddenly ill with a bad heart attack. I am just crying to God that he will raise him up again; he means so much to the work. Pray for him, friends! Surely God has still a great work for him to do among his own people. The 'Aggrey' of Lambaland (Doke 1931a, 3).

In 1933, as already stated above, Kasonga had the joy of leading Chief Kacheya to the Lord for salvation. The chief had been under conviction of sin and miserable for quite some time, but had been confused by the teaching of the Watchtower Sect. This cult had a stronghold in his area and was working hard to also convert him to their religion. Paul Kasonga, together with the missionaries at the mission, gave themselves to prayer. One evening, while Kasonga was at home, the chief arrived with his wife and told him that they wanted to yield their lives to Christ. Kasonga was overjoyed at this answer to prayer and sent a note with a boy immediately to Olive Doke so that she could share in his joy. I will let Doke recount this event:

> While I stood thus a little boy came up with a note from Paul the leper evangelist. I opened it and read, and my heart filled with a deeper praise and sang for joy. In it he told how our persistent prayers had been gloriously answered, and chief Kaceya had come at last to surrender to the Lord as his Saviour and Master; and not he only, but his wife. For months and months we have been asking this of the Lord, and he has graciously heard and answered (Doke 1933, 4).

One area that Kasonga was truly gifted in was that of counselling. At Kasonga's home, at any time of the day or night, you would find enquirers queued up waiting for their turn to receive counsel from his lips. Many backsliders were restored to the Lord through his patient personal instruction. Doke recalled one such incident:

> Then last week there came through the station a man who long ago had been one of our school boys and had come out for the Lord, been baptized, and joined the church. Then soon after he . . . had been attracted by the teaching of the Watchtower, . . . he came through the station and . . . When I suggested that he stay overnight and talk with Paul he eagerly jumped at it with the result that he found the Lord again that night, and went on his way rejoicing (Doke 1932, 5).

Many marriages that were on the verge of collapse, especially because of childlessness, were also restored after a couple of visits to his home for counsel. Some, who were already separated, were reunited as a result of his counsel. This was despite the fact that he himself never married because of his leprosy condition. One of Kasonga's friends, Shedeleki, wrote in *Paul the Leper*:

> He, with his wisdom, was instrumental in saving many marriages which would have come to divorce. Those who were determined to separate, after long conversation and prayer with Paul, have gone away in a different frame of mind, and, with God's help have kept together. They are with us today as happy families, living witnesses to Paul's loving tenderness and understanding, and yet persistence, in maintaining God's laws about marriage. (Doke 1955, 13)

At one time when all the missionaries left to go on furlough, Kasonga was left in charge of the entire station without a single missionary to supervise him. He found in Anasi Lupunga a kindred spirit and the two worked wonderfully together. They started prayer meetings in which they particularly prayed for the other professing Christians who were taking their Christianity lightly. By the time the missionaries returned from furlough they found a kind of revival had broken out in their absence. There was a greater seriousness about the things of God and a deeper spirituality among the people at the mission station. On her return to the mission, Doke wrote:

> It is lovely to come back and find how true and stalwart the Christians have been in one's absence, and how the faithful evangelists, Paul and Anasi, have not ceased to guide and teach insomuch that there has been a steady growing in grace and increase in attendance. They have realized God's power and presence, and are happy in his presence (Doke 1933, 2).

Doke also wrote in *Lambaland* in July 1934, "During my absence on furlough, the women's meetings were faithfully kept up by Paul the evangelist with an average attendance of about 18." The present Senior Chief Mushili Toili Lwebesha – Paramount Chief of the Lamba people – who formerly lived in Kafulafuta Mission, said during an interview for this thesis:

> Paul was known by the name of Kaputula. He was a fine Christian. He came to the mission to learn. He was a strong Christian. He counselled people. He strengthened the married couples. I used to help clean his house. He was a leper. Many of us were changed, and were different from others in the community, because of what we were learning from Paul. Sometimes, he used to be carried on stretchers (Lwebesha 2010).

Although it was not stated in Doke's reports that this was largely a fruit of her labours, it was. Frey reports:

> Miss O. Doke saw the need for more evangelists and therefore trained them during evening classes. Miss Doke involved herself in writing Bible notes to equip the local leaders with biblical material. She also took the evangelists around during the evangelistic treks, so that they had their training on the job. Those evening classes developed into three-week courses at Kafulafuta, which were extended to six weeks. The teaching was so essential, that church leaders were brought to the mission station for about six weeks for so-called 'in-service training', after which they were awarded with a certificate. These trainings went on for years. From 1939 onwards, there were some Bible School teaching sessions held and each course took 3 to 4 months (Frey 2009, 58).

The African leaders at the mission station knew that they owed a lot of their knowledge and inspiration from Olive Doke and so were determined to honour her for this. Kasonga led his fellow leaders in doing this. On

Sunday, 24 December 1933, after a morning service, Doke was taken by surprise when Paul Kasonga requested the congregation to remain behind to witness a presentation that the elders of the church were going to give Doke for her eighteen years of faithful service among them. Kasonga gave an account of Doke's faithful service and then handed her a letter of appreciation in the Lamba language signed by the elders of the church – these were; Paul Kasonga, Anasi Lupunga, Kelebi Mambwe Cintemfwe, Donald Kasangula, Ackim Kalasa, Andaba Cembo and Jonathan Matafwali. It read:

To whom we love, Walona Olive Doke,

> We, the members of the church at the Kafulafuta Mission, want to tell you that we love you very much because of your work in our midst. We thank God that he sent you to help us and live amongst us these eighteen (18) years. We pray that God may bless you abundantly and give you joy and send others to help.

One of the great sources of inspiration to the new African leaders was Olive Doke's courage and commitment to the work of spreading the gospel throughout Lambaland. Bob Litana recalled one of those trips when he accompanied Kasonga and Olive Doke. He wrote in *Paul the Leper*:

> We started in Lesa's country and then went on through Nduweni down to Machiya. Miss Doke and I stayed to have a meeting at Mukwangu, while Paul went on with his men to Shikayuni in Mukubwe's country. When he came back, we all started off on a long journey which took us through the forest with no villages, as we wanted to reach Fungulwe. We tried the shortest route as time had gone. But we lost ourselves and nearly died of thirst. We had to turn back to the Lufuwu River and camped there that night. Next day we got to Milambo following the banks of the river. Further on, Walona Doke got ill with fever. So I said to Paul that we ought to suggest to Walona that we return straight home because she was ill. But Paul said, "No, let us suggest that she go back with the

carriers. We will make a *machila* to carry her in; but we will stay preaching God's Word in the villages. But if you are afraid that she may get worse on the way, you go back with her and I will stay." When we went to suggest to Walona that she go back to the mission because she was ill, she refused, and furthermore, forbade us even to send a letter to Mr Cross, in case he insisted on her returning. She said, "Even if I die on God's journey, it is quite all right." Then Paul said, "That is a good answer, let us go to Lubwesya and rest a few days there." On that journey, a great number of people changed their hearts and numbers came asking questions of the things of God and the way of life. Sometimes we did not have time to eat. During those days, Paul very diligently taught the people. He was never tired of speaking of the things of God. (Doke 1955, 12)

Lions were among the most feared wild animals in the forest. From time to time they attacked the animals kept by the villagers and sometimes also attacked the villagers themselves. 1934 stood out in Olive Doke's memory as the year in which the nearby villages in the Wulima district were besieged by lions. A number of villagers were killed by these "man eaters" until the government sent hunters with guns who hunted them down. Thankfully, Doke and the other missionaries were not harmed by any of them. However, the fact that despite such experiences, Olive Doke remained labouring among the people of Lambaland was a great inspiration to them.

In the latter half of the 1930s, Paul Kasonga could no longer go with Olive Doke for the trips around the villages. This was because the leprosy broke out again on Kasonga's body. He again lost more of his body to this awful disease. Kasonga was largely confined to his house. Thankfully, in 1933 the mission staff had a new arrival, Sister Greening, whose medical knowledge enabled her to treat Kasonga's condition. Thus Kasonga was restored to health again, but he could no longer go on the long journeys out of the mission station. He had to be wheeled around on a bicycle in order to get around the mission station. However, his failure to go around the villages did not stop him from ministering to the churches all over

Lambaland. Where he could not go physically, he went through his letters. Elison Chimbila, who was a deacon in the church at Kafulafuta, became his scribe because Kasonga could not write very well, having lost his fingers. Kasonga wrote letters of encouragement or admonition or guidance and comfort to various churches and to various individuals in those churches who needed help right across Lambaland. It is a wonder how much God did through his servant despite his infirmity.

Slowly but surely the labours of the missionaries and the local leaders brought individuals to repentance and faith in Christ. Doke and Kasonga rejoiced greatly each time they were privileged to hear of a conversion among the people to whom they ministered. Writing in *Lambaland* in October 1934, Doke reported, "Next morning before we left two more came to change their hearts and I left Paul talking with them while I went on to the next village and gathered the people and had a service with them" (Doke 1934, 2). Some of those who were getting converted would have been among their fiercest opponents in earlier years. For instance, Doke wrote in the January 1935 edition of *Lambaland*:

> Paul is bubbling over with joy today! I thought something was up when I went down to Sunday School today and saw his face beaming. He could hardly wait to tell me his news. "Jimu Cheleka is even now in the vestry, he has come at last to give his heart to the Lord." Jimu, who is a nephew of old Chalwe, and a cousin to Sandawunga, Katanga, has for years done all he could to upset the work here, and perhaps Paul himself has suffered more than anyone at his hands (Doke 1935, 4).

When the time came for the missionaries to appoint their first indigenous elders at Kafulafuta, Kasonga was the first person they had in mind. His untiring devotion and his strong Christian character commended him to them for this office. So Kasonga, together with other Lamba men, were appointed as elders. They used to have their meetings twice a month in his home, where they dealt with all the issues related to the life and ministry of the church. It was a great relief for the missionaries who concentrated on other aspects of the mission station. Apart from preaching, Kasonga was also in charge of preparing young converts for baptism. Because of his poor health, and also because he put in so much time into the Lord's work, the church supported him financially through most of this time, even though he was not really in full-time employment in the church. He was greatly honoured and loved throughout the whole of Lambaland.

Doke acknowledged this in the April 1937 issue of *Lambaland*:

> For some time during the year, Paul was laid aside, but despite his weak body his heart has been strong in the strength which God supplies, and he has ever been the backbone of the work . . . These two who are also elders of the church are ever helping the weaker and more backward Christians and zealously watching over the purity of the church membership. It is their individual work which tells perhaps more than anything (Doke 1937, 1).

Although Olive Doke had a very amenable personality, especially with respect to the indigenous leaders like Paul Kasonga, she could also be stubborn. Patrick Litana, who was a young man in those days, said during an interview with respect to this thesis; "Doke was a tough woman who could not be deterred in any way when her mind was set" (Litana 2010). This aspect of her character became very evident in a long-running battle with the SABMS over relocation to Fiwale Hill, which lasted seventeen years. In 1934, the SABMS decided to move its work from Kafulafuta to Fiwale Hill. Doke could not see herself leaving her girls' school and so she totally refused to move. To make it clear that Kafulafuta was still alive and well, she ensured that a new iron roof was put on the church building in Kafulafuta late that year. When the Franciscan Fathers opened a girls' school next door at Ibenga, in 1936, this made Doke even more resolute at her determination to make her boarding school succeed. Hence, she remained in Kafulafuta, sometimes as the only European resident, when all the other missionaries had moved to Fiwale Hill. Thankfully, her two brothers, Clement and William, who were in active service among the Baptists in South Africa, supported her stand and wrote to the Baptist Union on this matter again and again. It would be wrong to conclude that

Doke was opposed to any missionary activity at Fiwale Hill. She encouraged it. She even laid the foundation stone for the first church building that was erected in Fiwale Hill on 21 May 1938, which was later replaced by the larger Phillips Memorial Church in 1950. The simple fact is that Doke did not want to leave Kafulafuta and the work she was already doing there. After seventeen years (1934–1951) of trying to move Olive Doke from Kafulafuta, and failing to do so, the SABMS decided to upgrade the girls' boarding school there instead. In fact, a new road was built between Kafulafuta and Fiwale Hill to improve communication. Any further discussion of the matter was postponed until after her retirement, which was due within the next seven to ten years.

The failure by the SABMS to move Olive Doke was partly due to what has since been termed "the Doke factor". The name "Doke" had become highly respected in missionary circles among South African Baptists. Bear in mind that Doke's parents had both died while trying to encourage pioneer missionary service in Central Africa. Also, remember that her brother, Clement Doke, had sacrificed immensely for the sake of Lambaland and was now the leading expert in Lamba grammar in the world. Yet, even Doke herself had become highly respected in her own right. For instance, in 1939 the Initiation Ceremonies Committee of the General Missionaries Conference entrusted Doke with the task of investigating Northern Rhodesian initiation ceremonies. This resulted in a lot of correspondence with various missionaries. She finally wrote a paper entitled, "Report of the Investigation of Initiation Ceremonies of Northern Rhodesia" in June 1944. This report is still extant in the Zambian National Archives. Doke had given herself to this work largely because of her commitment to the wellbeing of African women. In the report, she recounted the situation in various parts of Northern Rhodesia and rejoiced particularly at the success they had achieved in Lambaland in persuading the local people to do away with the custom. She wrote in her unpublished autobiography:

> Happily we in LAMBALAND in the Ndola district have arrived at the stage when the church members themselves realize that it is a definite evil and unnecessary, so that even the substitute ceremony that was instituted years ago has been

dropped. The elders feel that any parent in any way, to a lesser or greater degree, allowing their child to take part in such practices, should be disciplined. This was arrived at very slowly. As in other places the practice among the heathen now has been to cut down the period of seclusion and instruction for the initiate to a week or even a couple of days for convenience sake, and many have dropped it all together. The influence of the cosmopolitan population on the mines is responsible for much of this. They are being detribalized. But even on a 200-mile trek seldom does one see an initiate now, as in the old days, being led into the village shrouded in a blanket and then later decked out with a cap of beads woven into the hair. The old things are passing away (Doke 1944, 25).

Doke not only saw these initiation rites as an unnecessary evil, she also realized that only the gospel could rescue these women from the fears that bound them to the practices. Hence, she concluded her report by stating, "Only God in their hearts can cast out the awful fear which binds them to this custom. The spreading of the gospel of light and love is the only answer and solution to this problem. Let us not be discouraged but PRESS ON" (Doke 1944, 26). Happily, Doke's passion for the education and salvation of women soon paid off. In 1966, she was able to look back and write:

In those early days the women were very difficult to reach. They had always had a subservient position and were so dull of understanding that it seemed impossible to arouse them to realize that this message we had brought was for *them* as well as the men. What a different picture today. The women are taking their part in evangelization and there are many very fine speakers among them (Doke 1966, 7)

So, a woman who is being looked up to by such a wide section of missionaries beyond Baptist circles was no push over. The SABMS had their work cut out for them!

If, in trying to move Olive Doke from Kafulafuta, the SABMS did not appreciate what Doke was doing there, the wider Christian community did so. Winifred M. Pearce wrote an article on her in *The Christian* on 12 August 1948. Part of it summarized Doke's gospel endeavours during this period:

> For many years the only white person on the station at Kafulafuta, she was engaged largely in an itinerating ministry, travelling from village to village, in each calling the people together and in simple language telling them the gospel story. At the end of the day it was she who must take the gun and go forth in search of food for herself and her native carriers, their business being to set up the stockade within which her tent was pitched for the night and to build huge fires to keep wild animals at bay. When in the course of her travels rivers had to be crossed, neither danger nor difficulty could deter her, and by canoe, bark-boat, log bridge, or carried, she pressed on to deliver the life-giving message. Her small portable organ was ever an attraction, the first to hear the strains of music calling to their neighbours to come and see the lady with the dog-in-a-box who talked about God. In this way Miss Doke penetrated to places where no white person had previously been, often preaching eight or nine times a day. Such was the interest in the gospel that she aroused that in time it became necessary to institute 'hearers' classes, that those who had been influenced might receive further instruction. The demands upon human strength were so tremendous that, but for divine enabling, she must soon have broken down under the strain (Pearce 1948, 5).

It was not only the Christian community outside Lambaland that appreciated what Doke was doing in Kafulafuta and beyond, but, as we have already observed, the African leaders at Kafulafuta Mission honoured her when she clocked eighteen years on the mission field. They honoured her again in 1941. Paul Kasonga led the church to express their gratitude to her for the twenty-five years of service she had rendered among them. The young lady who had come among them when she was only twenty-five was now half a century old. A lot of her strength had been spent in labouring among them. Kasonga appreciated that and ensured that the church under his leadership made that known eloquently. As they had done in 1933, they again wrote a letter of appreciation to her, which they framed and gave to her. They then took a special offering, a thank-offering, in recognition to the Lord for his goodness in sending missionaries to their land and for allowing Olive Doke such a long period of service among them not only as a missionary evangelist but also as a missionary discipler. She had helped to build them into astute church leaders.

In the early years of Olive Doke's labours in Lambaland, she did a lot of the evangelistic preaching in the villages and also participated in the usual preaching in the churches. However, as local evangelists began to increase, she saw herself as more of a discipler.

> The members of the church would elect elders who would receive instruction from Miss Doke. They were very helpful and more instrumental in preventing divorces and reuniting couples by their sincere persuasiveness, gentleness and prayer . . . Any upsets in Christian families were noticed by the elders and they would always try to sort out the problems. The evangelists also came under Miss Doke's instruction and she was often thrilled to see an evangelist who had been in one of her school classes years before. These men were bastions of the faith as a result of their boarding school days, where they had received thorough grounding in the Christian faith, which enabled them to stand firm through thick and thin. A constant daily contact with the gospel was the most successful way of building up the faith (Meier 1975, 60).

This is what Carina Bellin found when she joined Olive Doke on the Lambaland mission field in 1938 and became one of her closest working companions for the next thirty-two years. Doke herself described their companionship thus: "Carina and I fit like two peas in a pod." This was partly because the two of them had a similar family background and Bellin began corresponding with Doke even before she got onto the mission field. Thus their friendship began before they even met. Although they lived in separate houses on the mission field, they often ate together and went on evangelistic treks together. By this time, these treks were being made on bicycles whereas previously Doke used to trek on foot. In these treks, Bellin concentrated on the medical and school side while Doke concentrated on the preaching and counselling.

By this time, churches had been planted all over Lambaland. Bellin describes how Doke was often called to sit in during church leaders' discussions of knotty issues related to church administration as they went from village to village.

> Miss Doke would be invited to 'sit in' on church cases and to take part in discussions on church administration during the weekend stopovers at the outstations. She was able to sit for hours and just listen – a gift that won for her the respect of the church leaders – as also that of being able to sum up affairs and give opinions regarding decisions to be made. Such a gift – or is it a discipline – is not possessed by many missionaries, male or female (Bellin 1973, 4).

Carina retired to Australia in 1970, leaving Doke behind in Zambia. Hudson Mwepe Mutembo, who was born in 1925, testified in answer to an interview for this thesis about the relationship that Doke had with Kasonga, and the way she worked with the leaders in private. He said, "Olive respected Paul Kasonga and considered him to be the head of the Mission. The two had respect for each other. They used to travel and preach together. They also met to eat together and to discuss matters together with other members of the committee" (Mutembo 2010).

In 1948, Doke Doke went on deputation work in England, where her family had originated about half a century earlier. While there, she wrote a letter which showed that while she was concerned about the immediate spread of the gospel, Doke had also been wisely laying the foundation for the church's future in Lambaland by continuing to work hard at the translation of the Bible into Lamba. Almost as an aside, you will notice the attachment that the church leaders, under Paul Kasonga, had to her. She wrote:

Dear Mr Bevan,

Just this minute I have finished typing the corrections for the Lamba Psalms, and hasten to send them to you, so that if possible they can be included when the printing of the Old Testament books is done. I had hoped to get them away sooner, but it has been impossible. Other things have come now to claim my attention. Because of my personal connection with Mr Gandhi many years ago, I have been requested from India to write an article for a book on his life, which is being published, and I find it a very difficult thing to do.

I'm on the eve, too, of leaving for deputation work in various places, and that means preparation.

I think I shall have to withdraw into a 'hermitage' if I am to get anything done in the way of language!!

I have had letters from the 'boys' in Lambaland, and they are begging me to come back quickly. They are so afraid that now that I have broken my leg my relations will persuade me not to go back to the field!! And in that event they say they would be as 'orphans'. They are like children, aren't they?

I'm afraid that you will think that there are a lot of corrections for the Psalms, but if you scrutinize the manuscript you will see that it is mostly the joining or separating of words and the capitals. There are very few real mistakes.

Obadiah and Isaiah I cannot tackle until I get back to the field where I have my proper references.

I do hope that you have had a profitable time with Canon Coleman. I am so disappointed to miss him out there, but I may see him again in London. Would it be possible to discuss with him about the publishing of the whole Bible, in the event of me finishing the translation of the Old Testament? Unfortunately I cannot give a time limit in which I could have it complete, but it will be the priority job. If he could give me something in writing to that effect, it would be helpful with my Society.

With kindest regards to you and Mrs Bevan, and greetings to the staff,

Yours in the Master's service,

O. C. Doke.

Finally, the missionaries felt it was time to ordain some men who were the fruit of their labours into the Baptist ministry of the Baptist Union of South Africa. The Rev Guyton Thomas conducted the ordination service in June 1953 and three men were ordained on that occasion – Paul Kasonga, Anasi Lupunga, and Bob Litana. Kasonga only served slightly over one year as an ordained minister in the Baptist church before he went to be with the

The picture above is the last photo of Paul Kasonga on the Sunday before he died.

Lord. His last sermon, preached from a wheelchair, was on Sunday, 18 July 1954. As he preached that Sunday morning no one knew that they were listening to his farewell sermon. His last Sunday on earth was actually two weeks later, on 1 August. It was communion Sunday and so the people were in from all the local churches in the area. Adamson Chilulumo preached a stirring sermon and Paul Kasonga gave the closing benediction, as he sat on his wheelchair. He had to be fed the elements of the Lord's Supper because he had no fingers. When the crowds dispersed, he asked that the missionaries take a photo of him. This surprised them because they rarely took any photos on Sunday. Little did they know that this was to be the very last photo to be taken of Kasonga in this life! On Monday, Kasonga felt unwell but felt much better in the evening. However, in the early hours of the morning on Tuesday, 3 August 1954, Kasonga quietly slipped into eternity in his sleep. That was how this servant of God entered into his eternal inheritance.

Although Doke had a very close relationship with all the three men who were ordained as the first Baptist pastors of Northern Rhodesia, she had had the closest relationship with Paul Kasonga, as we have already observed. For many years after his conversion, Doke went with Kasonga evangelizing in the villages. The two were so close to each other that the day before Kasonga died, Doke was busy nursing him with the hope that he would recover. It was not to be so. The following year she wrote his only surviving biography, *Paul the Leper – Apostle to the Lamba.*

Referring to the close relationship between Doke and Kasonga, Mrs Elena Spider Cosamu – a former resident of Kafulafuta Mission – said during an interview for this thesis, "Olive used to work with Paul. They worked together in all their work and they complimented each other. The spread of the gospel in Lambaland can be attributed mainly to the work of these two" (Cosamu 2010). Lydon Pensulo added, "Kasonga's death came as a heavy blow to Olive such that she entertained the thought of leaving the mission" (Pensulo 2010).

The death of Paul Kasonga was not the end of his influence among the people. He had poured his life into the lives of many other men and women. Thus, Isaac Lwambululwa (born 1938), presently of Mukolwe Village, in Fiwale, recalled during an interview for this thesis, "Paul influenced Lambaland with the gospel, and he was a mentor of many people who continued his work (Bob Litana, Mambwe Chintemfwe, Boas Mutwale, Lemon Kantu, etc.). These people kept the faith and lived it out" (Lwambululwa 2010).

4.5 Doke's Final Labours And Earthly Rewards

From this point onwards, we move on to see how Olive Doke's ministry as a missionary went on to its conclusion without Paul Kasonga. What we see is evidence that the world had taken note of this woman who not only laboured for the gospel in Central Africa, but was very sensitive and mature in her relationship with the indigenous people. Accolades began to be showered on her from literally every side.

1953, the year of the ordination of the first Baptist pastors, was also special to Doke in that she was to get an award she least expected. We will let her tell us what happened in her own words:

> The government sent to the mission a grant to be spent on school celebrations as well as a lot of flags and pennants for decorations. After the morning service at the mission station, buns, sweets and cold drinks were given to the people . . . As we were having tea we heard another car arriving and we were surprised to see the District Officer from Ndola, Mr Berwick. He said he would be pleased to join us at the church for a little while, and we all went down. When we got there I was busy with last minute preparations and did not notice the consultations going on at the back. After we had opened with a hymn and a prayer, it seemed quite natural that the D O should say a few words to the assembled company. Mr Holmgren interpreted for him, and it was some time before I woke up to the fact that he was saying something about me. He had come out to present me with the Queen's Honours Coronation medal which he proceeded to pin on me. I was

completely flabbergasted and have no idea what I said in reply
. . . (Kemp 1987, 88).

Four years later, in May 1957, she was to receive an even greater honour from the Queen – the much-coveted Member of the Order of the
British Empire (MBE). It all began with a surprise letter from the Private
Secretary's Office, Government House, in Lusaka, dated 8 May 1957. It
stated in part, "His Excellency the Governor has asked me to say that he
proposes to present to you at a ceremony to be held in the Park at Ndola
on the afternoon of Saturday, the 25th of May, 1957, the insignia of an or-
dinary Member of the Most Excellent Order of the British Empire, which
award was conferred upon you by Her Majesty in the New Year honours,
1957." This came as a surprise to this lady who was buried in the forests of
Africa! Her reply was characteristic of Doke who shied away from any publicity. Part of her reply read, "It will be convenient for me to attend on the
day mentioned, but to tell you the truth I would much rather that it were
just private." Her request was not granted, and so at a public ceremony on
25 May 1957, Doke was decorated with insignia of the Most Excellent
Order of the British Empire (MBE) – with all her transport and accom-
modation costs paid for by the State.

1957 was also the year that Doke, with the other translators, finished
translating the whole Bible into Lamba. She felt that her work was done
and so Olive Doke officially wrote to the SABMS asking that she be allowed
to "remain at Kafulafuta after her retirement – with no missionary salary or
status, just a small house – to carry on with translation work of her own"
(Kemp 1987, 88). Her interest was not in leadership but in ministry. She
still felt she had a lot to offer by translating books and booklets into Lamba
so that the wealth of the English language could be bequeathed to the
Lamba church. This was a very unique request. She was the only SABMS
missionary who, upon retirement, decided to remain at the mission station!
They did not know how to handle this. In the end they granted her request.
A house was built for her near the mission station.

Although Olive Doke's retirement from the SABMS was due that year
(1957), she was to remain a missionary until 1959. One reason for this delay was because yet another group recognized her leadership qualities and

example and asked her to take up a position of honour. In 1958, Doke was elected as the president of the South African Baptist Women's Association. During her year in office "she travelled 11,000 miles by car to visit the local South African and Rhodesia BWA branches, and also addressed Baptist women in England. She encouraged the women present to 'go forward' with God and re-dedicate themselves to serving God in a variety of ways, including that of mission work" (Kretzschmar 1996, 30).

4.6 Doke's Labours After Retirement

"When I first came to Lambaland, there was only one Lamba who could meet with us at the Lord's Table – but we praise God that at our recent Jubilee we gathered in his name a company nearly 600 and that was only representative." So wrote Olive Doke (Doke 1963, 4), almost fifty years after her coming to Lambaland. As she came to her year of retirement, she did so with a great sense of achievement.

Having retired, Olive Doke helped with the newly established Fiwale Hill Bible School, where she translated the lectures to the students and did some lecturing herself. She also continued with her writing and translation work. Her labours were greatly rewarded when the following year, in 1960, the entire Bible – Old and New Testament – came off the printing press in the Lamba language and was delivered to the Lamba people (Bellin 1973). Two years later she testified, "Translation on the whole Bible was finished in 1957 and in 1960 we were able to put it into the hands of the people with humble praise and thanksgiving that we had been privileged to complete this great and responsible work" (Doke 1963, 4). You have to hand it to her, that she played no small part in the creation of Lamba as a written language, quite apart from giving the Lamba people a Bible in their own language. That was an epoch-making achievement!

As she looked at the church that had come into being since she first set foot on Zambian soil, Olive Doke's joy in her retirement overwhelmed her. She had sensitively and maturely handed over the work to an indigenous leadership. She wrote in 1963:

There have been wonderful trophies of grace and strong and dedicated leaders have emerged who are now able to shepherd the flock. A New Testament church is established under the leadership of the Nationals whom God has called out; and it in turn is going out to others. Church government and finance is in the hand of the African himself, and God is blessing the work . . . The evangelistic work in the villages is now carried on by the African evangelists themselves and much more effectively than can be done by the Europeans . . . The two ordained ministers are doing a grand work as they have the oversight of the many village churches . . . It has been a wonderful experience to see the gradual working of the power of God through His Holy Spirit in the lives of those with darkened minds and hearts, and to witness their awakening. To God be the glory, great things He hath done. 'Not I, but Christ' (Doke 1963, 4).

Was Olive Doke ever lonely as a single woman in the heart of Africa? "I never felt lonely," she once told a journalist in 1965 (Jennings 1965, 38). "I am constantly being interrupted by people dropping in to chat. I have a great deal of work to do in translating and I have been given this long life to do it." The journalist went on to say, "Most people need the company of others; Miss Doke is not among them. Her life in the bush set her apart from others but it gave her self-sufficiency; she is complete in every way and needs no one." Earlier she wrote, "If she wasn't teaching at the mission she was trekking on her evangelistic work, or making roads or building. In her spare time she did translations. Among them are Pilgrim's Progress (never printed through lack of funds), the Bible, school books and religious booklets. Among the education texts is the *Reader*, still used in the mission schools today. She did her own printing as well – on two ancient hand-presses."

This is perhaps the best place to note the printing work that occupied so much of Olive Doke's time. The Kafulafuta Mission had a printing house, initially with one printing press which was obtained from England in 1925. Olive Doke learned how to use the press and later trained two men to operate it. In 1937, twelve years later, another printing press arrived. On a daily basis, Doke would not only translate and write books, but also see to it that these were printed and circulated across Lambaland. As noted earlier, some of these books, especially the school books, were purchased by the government and used in their schools across the Copperbelt Province where Lamba was the local language of the people. Many of the books and tracts produced were evangelistic in nature or meant to teach Christians the basics of the Christian faith.

Doke wrote a book entitled *The Life of Christ*, which was 300 pages long, with 74 chapters, dealing with the life of Christ. It was translated into Lamba and printed in England. It proved very helpful to the people in Lambaland. Other books printed, which were not necessarily religious, were those containing tales of Lamba folklore, history books concerning great African leaders and missionaries, and a specially prepared book on health suitable for African readers. Part of the hard work was the proofreading, which she did herself before breakfast.

> The method of printing was painstakingly slow. Only one typeface could be used at a time after the type had been set in the block. To print the following pages the set type had to be separated, the letters all sorted back into their boxes and then another type put together. One can clearly see that this must have taken up a large part of Miss Doke's time. She would have to produce printing material, whether by herself – which usually was the case – or by other missionaries, and then set the printing men to work. When the first page was printed, Miss Doke would have to check the type. If any errors were found, the incorrect letters had to be replaced and only then could the printing begin. The type would have to be inked manually after each leaf was printed (Meier 1975, 74).

One of the greatest proofs that Olive Doke had the right attitude and spirit towards the indigenous people was the way in which they respected her in the years leading up to and following Zambia's political independence. Those were very difficult times for anyone with white skin. When Zambia gained independence in 1964, national ties between Zambia and South Africa were severed and the SABMS had to withdraw all its missionaries. The years leading up to Zambia's political independence from Great Britain were not easy for missionaries. Anti-white sentiments were being expressed everywhere, including the mission stations. Chiefs too were influencing their people against missionaries. One missionary wrote back home saying, "Our young people, orderlies and nurses, school teachers and even more established church leaders, are being influenced by the cry for Independence and Freedom. Many do not understand what this might mean, but it is the cry of the hour" (Kemp 1987, 93).

The general feeling was that whites should leave, and many missionaries started leaving to go back to their nations of origin. The SABMS also decided to withdraw their missionaries. However, Olive Doke refused to go back home and the Zambian government allowed her to stay.

The rest is history. Doke's application was successful. She moved to a mine house in Luanshya, and she continued her labours for another eight years. She kept making her way back to Kafulafuta, where she had many ties with the local people. Her house servant who worked for her for some thirty-five years still lived there and so did some of her early trek carriers. Going to visit Kafulafuta was like going back home. On Independence Day, 24 October 1964, Olive Doke was asked by the new African political leaders, as the only woman honoured guest, to lead the procession into the Anglican Cathedral in Lusaka during the celebrations to thank God for Zambia's independence (Jennings 1965, 38). That is the high esteem in which the new Zambian government held her!

By the mid-1960s there were at least eighty churches in the villages as a direct fruit of the SABMS missionaries. In 1966, on the golden anniversary of Olive Doke's labours in Lambaland, the *Times of Zambia*, Zambia's leading newspaper, produced a full-page article on her on Monday 26 September. The editorial for that edition of the newspaper, which was entitled "Lifetime of Service" read:

> The word 'missionary' has a somewhat old-fashioned note today. Some churches have made an attempt to abolish it and find an alternative for independent Africa. Yet there is

no satisfactory substitute. Perhaps the attitude of the modern missionary has changed. The young volunteer workers who come to Africa are generally less concerned with teaching the Bible. They concentrate on providing technical and educational skills. Yet, it would be a great injustice to forget the achievements of the pioneer missionaries. They endured great hardships; many died for their beliefs. The schools they began were the training ground for most of Africa's modern leaders. This week we print an article on Miss Olive Doke, a missionary who has spent 50 years at Kafulafuta, southeast of Luanshya. At the age of 75 she can look back on a life of service. When Miss Doke arrived in this country, the Copperbelt was unheard of. David Livingstone had met his death on the edge of the Bangweulu swamps less than half a century before. Her first home was a mud hut. Olive Doke, still active and dedicated, is a link with an old tradition. She should be an inspiration to those today who believe in helping humanity (*Times* 1966, 1).

This was a secular newspaper that honoured her in this way.

Doke herself commemorated her golden anniversary as a missionary in Zambia with these words:

> My first words must be those of thanksgiving and praise and adoration to our Lord and Master in the midst of it all – there has not one thing failed of all His good promises. His daily presence, guiding hand and keeping power in all circumstances, have ever been with me. How I thank Him for wonderful health enabling me to do, far beyond the strength of woman, exploits for the extension of His kingdom among the Lamba people. At the time of my joining the staff of the SABMS, Northern Rhodesia, as Zambia was then known, was in 'darkest Africa' and little known to the outside world – now it is definitely 'on the map' (Doke 1966, 1).

She went on to talk about the changes that had taken place since her arrival in Lambaland:

> There have been tremendous changes in both country and people in these fifty years. From a people steeped in sin and witchcraft, by the wondrous power of God there has emerged a vast company of people whose lives have been changed by their acknowledgement of sin and acceptance of salvation through the cleansing blood of our Lord and are now serving Him by bringing others to take this same step by the preaching of the gospel.
>
> Many of these true saints of God have gone to be in the presence of their Lord whom they loved so dearly [she had individuals like Paul Kasonga in mind]. Others still have the privilege of serving him among their own people. Churches have been established and the responsibility is upon the shoulders of the many able leaders. Ministers have been ordained who take the oversight of the flock. Was it not to make the gospel of Christ to the saving of souls that we came? But with this ministry side by side is the medical work, which has developed from clinics to hospitals – and the schools designed to teach reading and writing in the vernacular so that the translation of the Scriptures could be of inestimable value to the converts. These schools are now taken over by the government and carried on to higher standards. The evangelists felt the crying need for further instruction in the Word of God and to this end the Bible School was started with a three-year course for the candidates. Many have passed through this and are now serving out in the field. The translation of the Bible into Lamba put the Sword of the Spirit into their hands and it has made mighty men of them – and women too. What hath God wrought! How great Thou art! (Doke 1966, 7)

Finally in 1972, at the age of 80, her health deteriorated rapidly due to a heart condition for which she had been on medication for many years.

Her frame could no longer hold the spirit that had laboured tirelessly for well over half a century. And so on 17 March 1972 she died quietly in her home in Luanshya. She was buried in Kafulafuta, next to the grave of Paul Kasonga, with whom she had laboured for her Master, the Lord Jesus Christ. Whether it was by her own request or by the initiative of the church leaders who handled the burial, it is evident that these two lives were destined to be together in more ways than one.

The Lamba women insisted that they would bury Olive Doke, and so they were permitted to fill in the grave themselves – something that had never been done before. This is how highly they esteemed their departed sister. An eyewitness of the funeral, Olive Sparrow, immediately sent this account of the proceedings to the editor of the *South African Baptist*:

> It was a beautiful morning on March 21, 1972, and many hearts in and around Luanshya, Zambia, awoke to the thought, 'Today is the day of Miss Doke's burial.' A simple coffin had been prepared at the small cottage hospital run by the mines in Luanshya, and the neatly built Baptist church had been well prepared by the daughters of the late Rev Anasi Lupunga. Several beautiful arrangements of flowers, gathered from the home gardens of friends who had loved Miss Doke dearly, decorated the church. About 100 people, African and European, gathered to pay their last respects to a great lady. Among those who were present was Senior Chief Mushili of the Lamba people. The service was conducted by the Rev G. W. Sparrow who based his tribute on the letters O-C-D (the initials of Olive's names), using them to describe some of the chief characteristics of our dear friend: Obedience, Consecration and Devotion.
>
> The coffin was carried from the church and placed in the mission vehicle by three African and three European brethren who had worked closely together with Miss Doke in the cause of Christ in Luanshya. We then proceeded to Kafulafuta Mission Station where a large gathering of people was waiting to greet their friend of so many years. The service in the

church was led by Rev Bob Litana who called upon others to give testimony to what Miss Doke meant to them and to the church over the years. It was a special privilege to have Mr Grenville Doke in the service, who was able to greet those assembled in the name of the Doke family.

At the close of the service, willing hands carried the coffin to the vehicle, as the girls from the school sang softly, and a procession was formed to follow the coffin down to the burial ground. There the Rev Les Haydon conducted the committal service assisted by the Rev Efelesoni Nkumbwa.

At this point the women from the church asked if they might be allowed to bury Miss Doke. And so, to the accompaniment of the singing of resurrection hymns, the women moved in to fill the grave and close the final resting-place of their beloved BaLona. Loving hearts laid wreaths and flowers on the grave. Thus with grief-stricken faces, but songs of hope on their lips, Esita, Tani, Elizabeti, Labeka and many others said their final 'syaleni-po' to Olive Carey Doke, Queen of the Lambas. (Sparrow 1972, 5).

The secretary of the SABMS wrote, "The passing of Miss Olive Doke, MBE, closes a chapter of missionary history in Zambia that is packed full of drama. Perhaps she is the last of the old school of missionaries who has gone to her eternal reward" (Kemp 1987, 104). The Rev W. T. Edmonds wrote a tribute soon after Miss Doke's death in the South African Baptist Magazine of May 1972 in which he sought to describe this gallant servant of Christ.

She lived alone but was not lonely; she had no 'higher education' but was called to teach the highest wisdom; she was naturally shy but was entrusted with the responsibilities of leadership; she did not desire publicity but was often called upon to be bold for her Master; she was every bit a lady but she was called upon to do 'a man's job'; she was often tired but she remained a devoted missionary to the very end (Edmonds 1972, 5).

In acknowledgement of her extraordinary labours, her tombstone reads, "Olive Carey Doke (1891–1972), Baptist Missionary (1916–1972), *balili-posele mukubaletela abalamba icebo iciweme caba Yesu Klistu*" (i.e. "she was committed to bringing to the Lamba people the gospel of Jesus Christ"). Thus ended the life of this remarkable woman – a triumphant close to a great life. We need to do something to reverse the present situation where, forty years after her death, there is still no definitive biography of Olive Carey Doke.

Two years after Doke died, her brother, Dr Clement M. Doke, presented over one hundred volumes of books on missions to the library of the Baptist Theological College of South Africa. This collection was called the "Olive Doke Memorial Collection" in honour of his sister's magnificent missionary service in Zambia. The South African Baptist Missionary Society also started the "Olive Doke Memorial Fund" which was to be used to assist missionary candidates in their training, preparation and research.

4.7 Conclusion

Why should the researcher be interested in these two lives? As has been shown, we have in the lives of Olive Doke and Paul Kasonga an example of true partnership between a pioneer missionary and an indigenous leader. We also have an example of a sensitive handover process that emphasizes the virtues of mutual respect and admiration, which this researcher argues are prerequisites to a God-honouring handover process in the work of missions. In the next chapter, the researcher proceeds to analyse this data to see how these virtues grew in the lives of these two individuals and how they became the bedrock on which the superstructure of the work of missions grew in Kafulafuta and across Lambaland.

CHAPTER 5

A True Example of Mutual Respect and Admiration

5.1 Introduction

In order for this researcher to arrive at lessons to be learned from the lives of Olive Doke and Paul Kasonga, it is important that the biographical sketch just presented in the previous chapter should be analysed. It is safe to say that from the number of independent primary and secondary sources, and both objective and subjective information, what the researcher has put together in the previous chapter is a fair reflection of the lives of these two persons and of their working relationship. He has not left out any information that would have materially changed this picture. Although there is likely to be some level of human error in the details, there has not been a single instance of information gleaned anywhere that has contradicted the picture that has emerged.

The analysis in this chapter is meant to go deeper than the narrative to see what may have prepared their lives for such a relationship of mutual respect and admiration, which facilitated for a formidable working relationship and sensitive and seamless handover process. It will also summarize the growing admiration as the two worked together for many years. Contrasts and comparisons will be made with other missionary-indigenous leader situations in order to bring the present case study into sharp focus. In this analysis, the researcher will emphasize the respect and admiration of the missionary (Doke) towards the indigenous leader (Kasonga) not because it was not mutual but simply because this research is about studying and justifying the sensitive transition from missionary to indigenous leader.

Reference has already been made to the differences between Olive Doke and Paul Kasonga that would have made their working relationship and the handover process of leadership in Kafulafuta difficult. "Olive was white but Paul was black. Olive was female while Paul was male. Olive was a missionary but Paul was a local person. Olive grew up in the comforts of the developed world while Paul grew up in a rural village. Olive enjoyed very good health but Paul was a sickly leper. One would expect a lot of problems between the two because of all these differences and yet they bonded together very well" (p. 20). Surely, this would have been a recipe for trouble, and yet evidence thus far shows that the two worked very well together.

Also, bearing in mind (as we saw from chapter 2) that at the time Olive Doke was coming into the mission field the attitude of paternalism was rife among missionaries, we ask what it was that made her different. Observe also that Olive Doke and Paul Kasonga were in leadership together for about a quarter of a century, one would have expected some serious fall-out at some stage, since superficial relationships tend to only last a short time, but this did not happen. It seems, from the data collected by this researcher, that the longer they worked together the more their mutual respect and admiration grew. How can this be explained?

5.2 The background of Olive Doke and Paul Kasonga

The researcher posits that the first explanation must be found in some details in the background of these two individuals. He, therefore, began there. It soon became apparent that, especially for Olive Doke, she grew up in a family environment that engendered the equality of all human beings irrespective of skin colour and economic status. It was more natural for Paul Kasonga because of the attitude of Africans generally to their white counterparts. This was evident in the biographical sketch.

5.2.1 The background of Olive Doke

The paternal grandfather of Olive Doke, William Knibb, championed the fight against slavery as a missionary to Jamaica. When her father, Joseph J. Doke, pastored in New Zealand, he fought for the cause of the marginalized Chinese. When he came to South Africa, he joined hands with Mahatma Gandhi to fight for the rights of Indians who were discriminated against. They say, "Charity begins at home." Doke learned lifelong lessons in her home as she saw her parents treating people of a different race with respect – against the very attitude that was prevalent in their own community. All this taught Olive Doke that a person's skin colour was not important. What mattered was that a human being was made in the image of God. Hence, where a person's character was admirable, his pigmentation was irrelevant.

Mulemfo, in wrestling with the reason why missionaries fall to the temptation of paternalistic superiority, stated that "a possible explanation is that the missionaries did not equate themselves as human beings on the same level as the missionized" (Mulemfo 2001, 11). This could not be said of Olive Doke. She saw herself as essentially the same as those to whom she had come to serve as a missionary. Three areas worth referring to as proof of this are:

(1) **Doke's relationship with her domestic servant.** The fact that Doke easily developed and maintained respectful relationships can be seen from the fact that she maintained her African domestic servant in Kafulafuta (and later, in Luanshya) for 42 years. Surely, that says something about the mistress' attitude of respect towards that servant. So, it was not just with Paul Kasonga that she maintained a relationship of respect and trust.

(2) **Doke's attitude towards African cuisine.** The effort Doke made to develop an acquired taste for the local foodstuffs as soon as she arrived on the mission field showed that she wanted to identify as soon as possible with the people. This was an attitude of respect for their culture and for them.

(3) **Doke's refusal to segregate.** Segregation on the mission field is a blindspot. It takes a very deliberate effort not to segregate yourselves as

missionaries from the indigenous people. This researcher has already referred to the time recalled by Hudson Litana during the interview for this thesis when Doke rebuked her brother Clement for segregation. Bearing in mind the possibility of error in that only one respondent to the interview brought this historical event to the researcher's attention, and that thus far there has been no collaborative evidence, it is still worth stating that this shows how sensitive Doke was to this. As Isaac Lwambululwa stated, "She considered herself as one of the indigenous people" (Lwambululwa 2010). This was why, when the chief's sister, Chalwe, became gravely ill, Doke could ask that she move in with her until she nursed her back to health. This is precisely what her father did for Mahatma Ghandi many years earlier. This helped Doke to look at Kasonga as if he was one of the missionaries too, and thus accepted his leadership on the basis of his spiritual stature and not on the basis of his skin colour.

5.2.2 The background of Paul Kasonga

For Paul Kaputula Kasonga, respect for the white missionaries was implicit. Hence, the phrase "Shikulu" and "Walona" attached to their names when calling them, which is literally "Grandfather" and "Grandmother" but is really the equivalent of "Sir" and "Madam", used to show respect.

5.3 The growing respect and admiration between them

5.3.1 Paul Kasonga distinguished himself

This researcher posits that the place that Paul Kasonga had in the eyes of the missionaries in general, and in the eyes of Olive Doke in particular, was not mere tokenism. He earned it. The researcher thinks that the general respect for indigenous Africans began to be nurtured into admiration for Kasonga even before 1920 when Kasonga disappeared from school and was only found during the itinerant preaching of the missionaries. They found that their young convert had already introduced Jesus Christ to the people in his village, despite the fact that he was battling with leprosy and had been segregated from the rest of the village. This must have left a very deep impression upon the missionaries.

The fact that Doke and Clement took Kaputula (i.e. Paul Kasonga) and Mose Katanga before 1920 to open a new school as teachers and preachers, showed that they had a growing respect and admiration for what the Lord was doing in Kaputula's life.

This growing respect and admiration became even more evident when, on Kaputula's baptism, they named him "Paul". What would have made them take the name of the most foremost apostle of the New Covenant and put it upon this young man? It would have been because of what they saw in him.

When "Chirupula" (J. E. Stephenson) asked for a teacher to start a school on his farm, it is not surprising that the missionaries immediately picked on Kasonga for this assignment. Kasonga worked so faithfully and so hard that Chirupula did not want him to leave. It took quite some persuasion by his brother, Peter, before he consented to Kasonga going away on holiday. Such a reputation would have reached the missionaries at Kafulafuta and hence increased their admiration for Kasonga by 1921 when he came back to the mission station for his first holiday.

Kasonga's spiritual stature also stood out when compared to other early converts under the work of the missionaries. For instance, when the economic boom came to Lambaland after the discovery of copper, a number of early converts backslid. Sandabunga, the very first convert that was baptized, who also became a translator and an evangelist, took on a second wife in 1926 despite his Christian knowledge. Yet, in all this period Kasonga was steadfast. Their respect and admiration for Kasonga grew during this period.

When it comes to admiration, it was the preaching of Kasonga that finally convinced people like Doke to make him a leader and the pastor of the church at Kafulafuta after his return from Chirupula. It has been noted in the biographical sketch that,

> . . . the people heard him gladly because he had a way with words in his mother tongue. No missionary could preach in Lamba as he did. Also, because he knew the mindset of his

own people, he used the sword of the Spirit to drive out sin from the darkest recesses of their souls in a way that no missionaries could. He used a lot of illustrations in his preaching. His stories made biblical truths come alive. One moment he would have the worshippers roaring in laughter as they saw the folly of their thoughts and customs, and the next moment he would use the same illustration to drive home very solemn truths with powerful conviction (p. 123).

If anything showed that the respect and admiration of Kasonga that the missionaries had was more for his spiritual progress than his outward personality, it was the state in which Kasonga was when leprosy had devastated his body. Kasonga was now walking on the stump that was left of his feet and only managed to hold a pen by putting it between the stump of his thumb and his palm. Someone else had to help turn Bible pages for him in order for him to read the Bible. Yet, this was the man they chose as the first leader of the Lamba church and the first indigenous leader at the mission station.

5.3.2 The working partnership of Doke and Kasonga

This researcher argues that it is one thing to respect and admire someone at a distance and it is quite another to respect and admire someone because you can see the sterling qualities in them as you work together. The respect and admiration that Doke had for Kasonga and that Kasonga had for Doke belonged to the second category. Doke and Kasonga worked as a team. Together with other evangelists, they travelled together on evangelistic trips through the villages. Every so often in the *Lambaland* periodical you read statements like, "In December, Paul and I had planned a trip to the village of Luwembe for the purpose of preparing some candidates for baptism . . ." (April 1931); "First about the journey that Paul and I were able to take after much delay . . ." (January 1932); "I had with me two evangelists, the ever-faithful Paul and Elison, a younger evangelist, but very promising . . ." (October 1932); "Paul and I had long talks with her [Chalwe] and pointed out what a real Christian should be in everyday life . . ." (April 1934); "As soon as the rains are over, Paul and I will be taking a journey up there

[Mukutuma Village] for a few weeks, and I believe the Lord is going to work very mightily there . . ." (April 1934). Doke and Kasonga formed a formidable team as they laboured together.

One of the biggest on-going works was that of translation. Although Doke had become quite fluent in Lamba by the start of the 1930s, she still needed someone who was better than her to see the various shades of meanings behind Lamba words to give her a second opinion. Kasonga fulfilled that role well. Hence, in the writing of *Kace-Kace* and the translation of the Bible, Doke and Kasonga worked closely together in a relationship of mutual respect.

Speaking about how Doke and Kasonga worked together, Lydon Pensulo said in a recent interview:

> They made a very good team. Their roles at ministry differed. Olive was more or less like a teacher, while Kasonga was a pastor-teacher and counsellor. More people sought for advice from him. Olive was much more respected than Kasonga. Olive would direct people to Kasonga for discipling. She would also identify spiritual needs among them and then tell Kasonga so he could address them. They worked as a team and cooperated very well between them (Pensulo 2010).

Enock Kabamba, also speaking during an interview for this thesis, said, "They depended on each other. Olive could not do anything without consulting Paul. She consulted Paul on the traditions of the Lamba people. She helped Paul to preach effectively. Olive was not a racist; she had a loving heart" (Kabamba 2010). Mulemfo explains the principle of reciprocal interdependence as a basis for genuine partnership. He writes, "Dependence in the body of Christ is dynamic and produces growth, leading to mature relationships . . . This is the dependence that Kasonga outlines where each member needs the other and is ready to give and receive. There is 'the mutual dependence of believers on one another' (Carson 1987, 42). The true dependence relationship that is: 'Under Christ, self-reliant and without prohibitive dependence will be in a better position to enter into reciprocal interdependence as a genuine partner. Mutual dependence, or interdependence, is the principle underlying all creation and all organised life, interdependence manifests relations of mutuality or reciprocity (Hintze 1980, 112)'" (Mulemfo 2001, 16). This is what you found between Olive Doke and Paul Kasonga.

5.3.3 Paul Kasonga's growing admiration of Olive Doke

This is, perhaps, the best place to acknowledge the fact that as the missionaries were developing a growing admiration for Paul Kasonga, Kasonga was also developing a similar growing admiration for Olive Doke.

To begin with, Kasonga and the other local leaders must have known that Doke had sacrificed a lot to simply be a missionary in their part of the world. With her capacity, she could have carved out a professional career back home in South Africa and minted some sizeable wealth for herself. Also, she had sacrificed the prospect of marriage and the raising of a family. Whereas some women have found spouses while on the mission field, these are the exception rather than the rule. Most women who go out single as career missionaries bid farewell to marriage too. This is because they are fewer single men among their fellow missionaries than they are back home. So, the fact that Doke remained single for the rest of her life was not a surprise. It was a price that she paid for the Lamba church. This evoked admiration from the Lambas.

Paul Kasonga and the other local leaders also saw Doke's resilience in spite of the challenges on the trips they made from village to village. She was not afraid of the wild and ferocious animals. Even when she was very weak due to ill health, they knew that it was difficult to convince her to go back. Thus, she was a great source of inspiration to them – especially that she was a woman.

That was why when Doke returned from furlough in 1933, she was given the surprise 'thank you' token by the church in Kafulafuta, under the leadership of Paul Kasonga. Although it has already been quoted in the previous chapter, it is worth repeating:

> To whom we love, Walona Olive Doke:
>   We, the members of the church at the Kafulafuta Mission,
> want to tell you that we love you very much because of your

work in our midst. We thank God that He sent you to help us and live amongst us these eighteen (18) years. We pray that God may bless you abundantly and give you joy and send others to help. (Greening 1934, 2)

Again, as already noted, this was repeated in 1941 when Doke had been on the mission for twenty-five years. Paul Kasonga again led this.

The picture above shows Olive Doke standing, with Paul Kasonga and Anasi Lupunga holding the framed certificate they had signed in honour of her

5.4 Kasonga's leadership finally acknowledged and earned

5.4.1 Kasonga's admirable leadership and pastoral skills

Since this is an analysis that justifies the handover of leadership of the church and mission to the indigenous leader, Paul Kasonga, it is only right that the researcher should end it by showing that Kasonga earned this leadership. Again, the historical data seems to show that Kasonga earned this position due to the admiration that the missionaries had for him.

Kasonga's leadership skills were proved when all the missionaries left on furlough and he was left in charge of the mission station. By the time the missionaries returned they found everything in order and a deeper spirituality among the people. The missionaries returned and realized as never before that they could leave him as overall leader. Kasonga was a very capable man.

Doke's respect for indigenous leadership was not limited to Kasonga. She respected these men that she had discipled and was willing to sit tight-lipped among them as they invited her into their discussions, and would only speak upon being invited to do so. Bellin's testimony, referred to in the biographical narrative, is an important eyewitness account. She said that Doke would sit for hours and just listen. "Such a gift – or it is a discipline – is not possessed by many missionaries, male or female," (Bellin 1973, 4). This was because Doke brought herself down to the level of fellow worker with these men. She was not riding over them with the airs of a missionary.

It is possible for someone to wrongly conclude that on Doke's part this deference to Kasonga's leadership (and that of the other men) was simply because she was female. Nothing would be further from the truth. Doke could be stubborn if she was not convinced about something, and she would defy orders even if they were coming from a white male! A case worth citing was that of the orders from South Africa that all the missionaries should leave Kafulafuta and move to Fiwale Hill in 1934. All the other missionaries moved except Doke and her chief reason for defying orders was that she did not want to abandon her girls' school. This defiance lasted seventeen years, until the SABMS gave up. So, it cannot be said that it was simply her effeminate disposition that made her acquiesce to

Kasonga's leadership. It was because she genuinely admired his leadership and respected it.

The missionaries at Kafulafuta not only saw Kasonga's pastoral skills at the home mission, but also across Lambaland. It was noted in the biographical sketch that when Kasonga was unable to travel due to the ravaging consequences of leprosy, he remained at the mission station and did not go on evangelistic trips any more. However, with the help of Elison Chimbila, he was able to write letters of encouragement and admonition, of guidance and comfort, to various churches and individuals across Lambaland. He was greatly honoured and loved throughout the land. This pastoral heart was commendable. Hence, it is not surprising that in 1931 Kasonga's name appeared on the cover of the Lambaland newsletter together with that of Olive Doke as a fellow leader of the Kafulafuta Mission. Also, when the time came for them to appoint the first elders of the church at Kafulafuta, Kasonga's name was the first on the minds of the missionaries. And, similarly, when the time came for them to ordain the first pastors in 1953, Kasonga's name was among the three that were chosen – again, despite his medical condition.

5.4.2 "The 'Aggrey' of Lambaland"

This researcher took note of Olive Doke's reference to Paul Kasonga as "The 'Aggrey' of Lambaland" (*Lambaland*, April 1931), and investigated who this Aggrey was. It soon became apparent that this was yet further proof of the admiration that Olive Doke had for Paul Kasonga. A very short biographical sketch of Dr James Emmanuel Kwegyir Aggrey (1875–1927) should suffice to prove the point.

Dr I. S. Ephson, summarized the life of Dr Aggrey thus:

> One of the leading figures in the history of education in Africa was undoubtedly Dr James Emmanuel Kwegyir Aggrey, more popularly known as 'Aggrey of Africa'. Noted as a great sociologist, orator, preacher, and far-sighted a politician, and equally famous for his witty and epigramatic sayings, Aggrey, an apostle of inter-racial co-operation, advocated and helped to cut the path of progress for the African race in many fields,

particularly in the direction of religion, education, and agriculture (Ephson 1969, 2).

Aggrey was born in 1875 in the Gold Cost (present day Ghana), in West Africa, and soon distinguished himself in the realm of education. He became a pupil teacher in different schools and soon rose to the position of headmaster of the Wesleyan Memorial School. He sat for the Teachers' Certificate examinations and came out first among 119 candidates from across the whole country, enabling him "to teach in any similar school in any British Colony, the world over."

Aggrey briefly became a politician and a soldier between 1895 and 1898. For the next twenty-six years, Aggrey relocated to the United States of America, where he married and had two of his three children. While in the USA he obtained two doctorates and was ordained as an elder in the Methodist Episcopal Zion Church. He returned to West Africa in 1924 and joined the teaching staff of Achimota College.

In the last three years of his life, Aggrey toured Africa as part of the Phelps-Stokes Fund Commission for the education of Africans. He was in Sierra Leone, Liberia, Nigeria, Cameroon, Belgian Congo, Angola, Kenya, Uganda, Tanganyika, Zanzibar, Nyasaland, Rhodesia, South Africa, etc. Ephson records, "In South Africa, he so much impressed the white settlers at public lectures that his audience wildly and admiringly exclaimed, 'Damn his colour, he's a saint'" (Ephson 1969, 5).

Aggrey championed holistic education that trained the head, the hand and the heart. He wanted both boys and girls to be trained. Aggrey said, "No race of people can rise half slave, half free. The surest way to keep a people down is to educate the men and neglect the women. If you educate a man you simply educate an individual, but if you educate a woman you educate a family" (Ephson 1969, 5). In this he obviously won Olive Doke's heart and admiration.

Aggrey also laboured to improve the economic livelihood of the African people, whether in the USA (the African Americans) or in Africa. In the USA he encouraged the formation of African American associations and banks in order for the African Americans to free themselves economically.

In Africa, he toured the Gold Coast encouraging agriculture as a means to improve the economy of the people.

At a time when inter-racial tension was very high, Aggrey laboured for inter-racial harmony. He wanted each race to be proud of who they were while at the same time seeking friendly relations with other races in an ambience of political equality. He advocated for this wherever he went. In 1919, he felt that Africa was the Sleeping Beauty of the world and that she would soon wake up from her centuries of sleep. He had great hopes for Africa.

Aggrey died in 1927, during a brief visit to England and the USA. He was mourned in all the continents. Ephson states that his pallbearers were all distinguished white citizens of the USA and that in his own country, the Gold Coast, every town and village observed his death with weeping and mourning.

It is this Aggrey that Olive Doke likened Paul Kasonga to four years later. This can only speak about the great admiration she had for him.

Perhaps the final proof of Doke's admiration of Kasonga lay in the fact that she wrote his only surviving biography, *Paul the Leper – Apostle to the Lamba*.

5.5 Conclusion

In this chapter, the researcher analysed the lives and relationship of Olive Doke and Paul Kasonga, using the data brought together in the previous chapter. The analysis shows a relationship that grew in mutual respect and admiration over the quarter of a century when they laboured together. This could not have been easy, in the light of the many differences between the two individuals. Credit, therefore, needs to be given to their godly spirituality – both of them. And it was this ambience in their relationship that led to the seamless handover process that took place in Kafulafuta. In the light of this analysis, we are now in a position to work on a model or strategy to help us achieve something of this relationship of mutual respect and admiration in order for us to achieve God-glorifying handover processes on the mission field.

CHAPTER 6

Transforming Paternalism into Partnership: Application

6.1 Introduction

In this chapter, the researcher will discuss the pertinent lessons learned from the relationship between Olive Doke and Paul Kasonga. This is by way of working towards a model that is meant to help us transform the current relationships of paternalism and suspicion that are so common between missionaries and indigenous people into those of mutual respect and admiration. The researcher will use an inductive approach to go from these two role models and propose some actions to be taken in order to ensure that when the terminus of missions is reached in any mission situation there will be a smooth handover.

6.1.1 Lessons for the African church

As this researcher works on a model that can be used to ensure a smooth handover process in the work of missions, it is important to emphasize that this is not motivated by a desire to see Western missionaries leave Africa. Rather, it is meant to be a lesson to Africans as the baton of missions is handed over to us. The researcher stated in the first chapter that African Christians are best poised to take the gospel to the areas that still remain the least evangelized on the planet; namely, the 10/40 window and Africa's own rural areas. As the African church rises to this challenge, there is a need to ensure that the mistakes of the past are not repeated. Since one area beset with painful experiences is that of the handover process from missionaries to indigenous leaders, the African church should ensure that any such future endeavours are spared of such pains and sorrows.

So, the model being proposed is for the African church to use as it takes up the baton of missions and runs with it. Our indigenous missionaries will need to go into Muslim countries and into rural areas with the gospel. They need to be conscious of the danger of paternalism and suspicion. Bad relationships on the mission field invariably become a bottleneck to the work. A lot of energy is lost in internal firefighting, which could have been spent in expanding the borders of the work.

However, much more than that, they need to arm themselves with the tools that will ensure that they develop patterns from the very beginning, which will ensure true partnership with the indigenous leaders whom they will bring up under their ministries. That is what this chapter is all about. What is being presently expected of foreign Western missionaries will be expected of the African professionals who will become missionaries as well. As Mulemfo stated, "There is no guarantee that Africans would not also commit mistakes in their missionary endeavour" (Mulemfo 2001, 11).

6.1.2 Researcher's interest is pastoral

Hence, the researcher wants to state again that his interest is not merely historical but primarily pastoral. This is not merely a documentation of what happened in the past, but an effort to learn from that past in order for the church to do a better job in the future. The researcher is looking for a model that he can apply to his own church's missionary endeavours so that the mistakes of the past are not repeated. He looks forward to seeing the fruit of this model in a successful terminus point for the churches being planted by missionaries being sent out from his own church. That is the heart of this research and hence the importance of this chapter.

It needs to be understood that the good example between Doke and Kasonga is rather unique, especially because there was no deliberate training to bring this about. But for us, there is need to ensure that we come up with a system that may produce such results. Below, then, is a proposed structure to be worked out to foster a relationship of mutual respect and admiration between missionaries and indigenous leaders on the mission field.

6.2 Missionary training and orientation

If mutual respect and admiration is going to be found at the mission station, it must be found in the context where missionaries undergo training and orientation. It was observed that Olive Doke received this training in the context of growing up in her parents' home. Her father, by his example, fostered in her a respect for the rights of minorities and marginalized peoples. She learned to see them as being equal with her simply because they were made in the image of God. She learned to admire people like Mahatma Ghandi, despite the fact that he belonged to a lower class of citizens in her own country. This was both training and orientation for her, since it was taking place on the continent where she was to labour.

6.2.1 A curriculum that teaches human equality

However, not all missionaries will have this privilege. Hence, it is important that in the curriculum of missionary training, there must be lessons that open their eyes to human equality in the eyes of God, despite the outwards backwardness they would find in the mission field. Biographical studies of indigenous leaders among the people among whom they are going to work should be included in the curriculum. Hence, it was because of her acquaintance with the great Dr Aggrey of West Africa that Olive Doke would look at the leper, Paul Kasonga, and with admiration, refer to him as their own 'Aggrey'.

6.2.2 Stories of successful handover processes

Other biographical studies should include successful handover processes. Sadly, very, very few biographies of missionaries deal with this. Many of them simply show how the pioneer missionaries laboured until they died, without highlighting the sensitive handover process. Instead of going on to show the kind of persons that the missionaries finally handed over the work to, the biographies tend to hide them in the shadows and simply continue with the missionaries up to their death. They then summarize the missionaries' achievements. This needs to be rectified. Hence, examples like that of Olive Doke and Paul Kasonga should be essential reading during the training stage.

6.2.3 Authentic orientation in cultural understanding

Part of what fosters paternalism is that not only is the training done in the country where the missionaries come from, but often the material used to understand the culture in which the missionaries go to work is paternalistic in describing that culture. The missionaries, therefore, go with preconceived ideas that rob them of the ability to appreciate the richness of the culture in which they are going to work. The view that Africans are 'raw savages' (to borrow Lumba's statement, see p. 55), which many Western missionaries once used to go with into the African mission field, is not entirely exorcised out of them.

So, some orientation on the mission field (or at least through the eyes of indigenous Christian leaders) is vital to ensure that missionaries understand the inner life that lies behind the cultural practices that look very strange to them. This is to help the missionaries avoid the error of "throwing away the baby with the dirty bath water". As Bill Taylor warned, "Some leaders, operating with their mono-cultural framework of values and behaviour, end up imposing themselves, subconsciously regarding their partners as junior, or secondary, players" (Moreau et al. 2004, 376).

6.2.4 Understanding the stages of missions work

Having seen what should be involved in the training and orientation of missionaries, we must now move on to consider what should be involved in the actual process of church planting that will remove the spirit of paternalism and suspicion and instead foster a spirit of mutual respect and admiration. The researcher stated in his first chapter that, "the success in planting the Baptist denomination in Zambia was not accidental. It was because of the dedication *and deliberate strategy* of those who laboured during the pioneer stage of the work" (p. 7). This deliberate strategy is the process that we must now consider.

The best way to proceed is by dividing the process of church planting into the three phases that were stated in chapter 1 (see p. 71): (a) the initial phase of evangelism and discipleship when the missionary is providing the leadership alone, (b) the second phase in which the missionary shares leadership with indigenous leaders and is largely grooming them to take over the work, (c) the final phase in which the missionary hands over top leadership but is still involved with some leadership role before finally totally disengaging.

In an interview for this research done with Rev Isaac Chimfumpa (who has worked with Western missionaries for over 50 years), he divided these into four stages. He said:

> Stage 1: Pioneer (missionary) – Mission role – as a pioneer he needs the gift of leadership along with other gifts. There will be, to begin with, no local believers. The missionary must do much of the work himself.

> Stage 2: Parent (missionary) – The missionary requires the gift of teaching. The young church has a growing child's relationship to the mission. But the 'parent' must avoid paternalism.

> Stage 3: Partner (missionary) – The missionary changes from 'parent-child' relationship to 'adult-adult' relationship. This is difficult for both the missionary and the national leaders but it is essential to the church becoming a mature 'adult'.

> Stage 4: Participant (missionary) – A fully mature church assumes its own leadership. As long as the missionary remains, he should use his gifts to strengthen the church to meet the original objectives of Matthew 28:19–20. However, he should be involved in stage 1 elsewhere (Chimfumpa 2010).

Even before we proceed to look at this, it is important to state here that some missionaries arrive on the mission field without this 'road map'. They see themselves as career or life-long missionaries (which is fine), but they mistake this for being the overall leaders until they die. The two are not the same. As already stated in the first chapter, missions must have a terminus. The terminus must be the handing over of the work to local leaders so that self-governing, self-supporting and self-propagating churches can be realized. The missionaries must have a road map as to how they will get there. This road map must be informed by the Bible, which has principles that are for all places and for all time. So, this three-phased road map is helpful for any missionary to follow.

6.3 The first stage of missions

This first phase of the work of missions is inevitably paternalistic in some way. The missionaries come to teach the local people what they do not know. They come as parents to children and give them the first principles of the Christian religion. In times past, the missionaries often also had to reduce the language of the indigenous people into a written language and then teach them the basics of literacy.

The researcher showed this legitimate and strategic 'paternalism' of this first stage from the example of the Lord Jesus Christ and also from the example of the apostles. They brought the gospel to a people who did not know the message and so they considered themselves stewards of this message. They were the ones who had the Holy Spirit, and sought to share his power with the people to whom they came. This is legitimate paternalism and must not be frowned upon.

This first stage involves both the work of evangelism and the work of discipleship. The missionaries are the sole leaders and everyone who is converted is a follower. The missionaries bring the knowledge, skills, and funds to the mission field and seek to share the fruit of all this with the people to whom they have come. What should happen in this very early stage to ensure that this paternalism is not entrenched?

6.3.1 Imparting a worldview that kills paternalism

The missionaries must humbly and deliberately impart a worldview to those who are being evangelized and discipled that does not encourage a paternalistic relationship. In order for them to do so, they will need to have an incarnational approach to missions that enables them to be seen as 'one of us' by the indigenous people. As Wickeri (*Missionalia* 2005, 506) rightly concluded about Allen's book, the missionaries must have a self-emptying and negation attitude as they go about their work.

6.3.2 Contextualizing the gospel message

They will also need to contextualize the gospel so that the people they are evangelizing and discipling understand it in their own thought forms. This demands abilities in cross-cultural communication that are often the preserve of those whom God has called to missions work. Only where this is done will the indigenous people lose their inferiority complex and relate to the missionaries and their message as their own. This makes the handover process later to be less traumatic.

6.3.3 Training the people to critic their culture

The missionaries also need to disciple the local people so that they can critique their culture from the Bible's perspective and not from their own culture's perspective. This is by passing on to them a comprehensive biblical worldview, so that even in areas that the missionaries have not taught them, they will be able to think for themselves and apply biblical principles. In this matter, the missionaries must lead by example. Before their very eyes (and ears) they should critique their own culture using the Bible as the reference point. It is this, which will engender true admiration from the missionaries as they see them work out their understanding of the Bible in the challenges they face in their own culture and also in shepherding others in the next stage of missions.

6.3.4 Training the people to think for themselves

During this discipleship process, the missionaries need to make their disciples less and less dependent on them, and more and more dependent on the Scriptures and the Holy Spirit. Whenever the people ask the missionaries about anything, like the Lord Jesus Christ, they should ask the question, "What do the Scriptures say?" And once they give the correct answer, the missionaries should tell them, "Go and do likewise." They should believe that the same Holy Spirit who has inspired and guided them will also inspire and guide their disciples. As Allen (1991, 144–145) says, he will also teach them "true conceptions of morality, doctrine, ritual." As the disciples of the missionaries become more independent of them and more dependent on the Holy Spirit and the Scriptures, there will be times when they will make mistakes. The missionaries should give them the space to do so, and then come alongside them to gently correct their thinking – again by using the analogy of faith in the same Scriptures. This will mature their sense of responsibility and correct use of the Bible.

It is worth listing afresh at this point the mistakes often made by partners as warnings about mistakes that the missionary to be wary of. Daniel Rickett (Moreau 2004, 286–287) gave this list in a slightly different context but its warnings are relevant to the missions enterprise especially when it is in a different culture:

Mistake 1: Assuming you think alike

Mistake 2: Promising more than you can deliver

Mistake 3: Taking to the road without a map

Mistake 4: Underestimating cultural differences

Mistake 5: Taking shortcuts

Mistake 6: Forgetting to develop self-reliance

Mistake 7: Running a race with no end

It is a failure to be mindful of these that inadvertently frustrate the maturing of disciples into independent fellow leaders at the right time. The researcher brings this list here because mistake 6 is about failing to help the people to become independent.

6.3.5 Fostering a spirit of mutual respect

It is important that a spirit of mutual respect is fostered at this stage, with the missionaries showing that we are all made in the image of God with equal capacity to know and understand his will under the direction of the Word of God and the Spirit of God. It is this spirit of mutual respect, which will be a foundation for mutual admiration in the second and third stage below. Without this, frustration is just waiting to happen. Where mutual respect has been fostered, there will be strong relationships and godly interaction, which will produce genuine and wise partnerships in the leadership team.

This is what made Olive Doke really admire Paul Kasonga as he helped married couples who were about to divorce despite the fact that he himself was not married. He had learned the principles in the Bible and was applying them to the situations that came before him in a way that, perhaps, Doke herself could have never done.

6.4 The second stage of missions

This second stage of the work of missions is about shared leadership, with the missionaries growing into the position of being "the first among equals" (Strauch 1995). Whereas paternalism may have had legitimate boundaries within the first stage, it is totally out of bounds in this second stage. This was again proved from the example of the Lord Jesus Christ and from the example of the apostles. Whereas in these two examples there was an almost perfect handover, on many mission fields this is where trouble begins. The spirit of paternalism continues unabated on the part of the foreign missionaries, while the newly chosen indigenous leaders are characterized by a spirit of distrust and an inferiority complex.

6.4.1 Rooting out the wrong attitudes early

One reason why the researcher has emphasized what he did in the first stage of missions was in order to root out this spirit in both missionaries and indigenous leaders even before they come together into a context of shared leadership. Often, these problems are latent and unaddressed in the first stage and consequently rear their ugly heads when power is shared. So, the missionaries must ask themselves the question, "How much have I done to humbly bring myself from the 'missionary pedestal' in my work of discipling these men? How much have I done to change their worldview so that they can see me as an equal, whom they respect at that level and admire simply because of the gifts that God has bestowed upon me?" These questions must be asked and answered honestly because as long as the inferiority complex continues, as Lumba rightly observes (1995, 45), the national leaders will continue to think that they can never do what the missionaries are able to do.

6.4.2 Identifying persons to groom into leaders

In this stage of the work, the missionaries would have identified the persons with the rudiments of leadership gifts and began to disciple them with an eye on finally ordaining them into full-fledged elders. In fact, it is from among these individuals that the future overall leader of the work may be finally chosen. A lot of care has to be taken to ensure that those being chosen are properly qualified because the future of the church hangs on this matter more than any other. It was evident that Olive Doke and the other missionaries with whom she worked took their time to finally arrive at their choice of men for leadership, hence the strong foundation that was laid for the Baptist church in Zambia. It took no less than ten years before Paul Kasonga made it into the top leadership of the mission in 1931, and it took another twenty-two years before he was ordained as a pastor – together with Anasi Lupunga and Bob Litana.

The missionaries must choose individuals whom they respect and admire. The emphasis in this respect and admiration must not be in outward appearances or positions held in society, but rather it must be in their spiritual maturity and levels of giftedness for the work of ministry. Again this is very evident in both the example of Scripture (as many of Jesus' disciples were uneducated and unsophisticated fishermen) and in the choice of Kasonga (a leper) to lead the work in Kafulafuta. As the researcher wrote in the introduction, "The fact that the early missionaries chose a leper to be the first official local leader of the church is in itself worth stating, studying, and possibly even commending. Like God, whom they sought to serve, they looked at the inward person and not at the outward man, which was being eaten away by that dreaded disease" (p. 13).

There should be no hurry or shortcuts at this point. If no persons are coming up through the ranks with admirable gifts and growth, the missionaries should not simply appoint them for the sake of sending good reports back to their sending churches. Many missionaries know that the lack of quick results can be a cause of anxiety from the missionaries and their sending churches. The temptation to push anyone into the ranks of leadership can be very high.

Whereas some missionaries tend to move too quickly and then burn their fingers, others move too slowly and cause a lot of frustration in the process. The researcher stated earlier that, "In certain cases, the foreign missionaries have outlived their welcome. They have overstayed and clung on to leadership for too long" (p. 37). So, whereas there is no biblical timeframe in terms of specific number of years, the missionaries must be sensitive to the maturing process of the people whom they are nurturing for leadership and yield ground to them accordingly.

The fact that missionaries have a number of good solid persons in the leadership should not cause them to squeeze in someone who is unspiritual. It only takes one rotten groundnut to mess up the rest that are in the mouth! The immature and worldly leader will spoil the spiritual atmosphere in the leadership team and foster suspicions until the innocent minds are polluted. So, the missionaries should only appoint into the leadership team those who are showing admirable gifts and graces. No tokenism please!

In an interview for this research, Manasseh Kaonga (who had worked under foreign missionaries for over fifteen years) spoke about the need for indigenous leaders to prove themselves. He said, "Nationals need to prove themselves that they can be trusted to spearhead the work successfully. They must display integrity and responsibility. There should be no competition for attention and loyalty must not be to a missionary but to God alone" (Kaonga 2010).

6.4.3 Delegating leadership responsibilities

Part of the responsibility of this stage is to share out the various responsibilities of overseeing the development of the work. The leadership team should come together fairly often to share about the work and to plan for it. The missionaries should defer matters brought to their attention to the other leaders as much as possible. In this way they will be preparing for their own departure from the scene. Their interest should be in hearing about how they have handled such matters, to see whether biblical principles have been rightly observed with the help of the Holy Spirit. Where one or two leaders are distinguishing themselves in their work, admiration will inevitably grow towards them.

The missionaries should not hold anything back from the indigenous leaders – not even information about finances. They should not create a dichotomy between what the indigenous leaders can handle and what the missionaries (alone) can handle because they are the missionaries. To do so is to continue a paternalistic relationship under a thin veneer of partnership. Remember, the missionaries are working themselves out of a job. Hence, by slowly but surely bringing themselves to the same level as their team of leaders, it will be easier for the missionaries to finally work under them or even to leave and go elsewhere to continue their ministry.

6.4.4 Spending much time with the leaders

The missionaries must make it a deliberate policy to spend a lot of time with their fellow leaders. Time together builds deep relationships. Part of this time will be inevitable as meetings are called to discuss various matters related to the work. However, the missionaries must also seek other times when their lives can be in full view of the other leadership team members. Thus they will see how they handle challenges that confront them at a personal level and they will also see how they handle their challenges. This will foster mutual respect and admiration.

This spending of a lot of time together was evident from the example of the Lord Jesus Christ, who spent three solid years eating, sleeping, and ministering with his disciples. It was also evident from the apostles who formed apostolic teams with those who made up the next generation of leaders and laboured together with them as they went from city to city. It was also evident from the relationship of Olive Doke and Paul Kasonga. They spent a lot of time working and travelling together.

6.4.5 Passing on the vision for the work

Where the vision of the work has been appropriately passed on to the indigenous leaders, they can run with it without constantly looking back to see if they are heading in the right direction. This vision must be biblically based so that the Bible remains the organizing principle of the whole team. Hence, the missionaries must teach the leaders what the common objective is (i.e. the Great Commission) and thus they can all work together with some sense of individual independency towards achieving optimum fruitfulness in this institution called 'the church'.

In an interview for this research, Manasseh Kaonga touched on this very matter. He wrote:

> The missionary must define the vision of his work and deliberately begin to share it with nationals. A missionary must understand that he can never be a true substitute to nationals, hence can never build any lasting work without involving nationals. He must stop being dictatorial, but begin engaging nationals deliberately to become innovative and creative. When the national is matured spiritually and shows readiness, the missionary must never hesitate to transfer true authority to the national. . . . Mistakes by one national must not be used against other innocent nationals. Missionaries must have faith and trust in the nationals who can think competently (Kaonga 2010).

6.4.6 Encouraging leaders to use their gifts

The missionaries must also encourage the leaders to use their gifts to the maximum so that their own admiration for their levels of giftedness is genuine as the missionaries see what they are able to do beyond their own abilities. The self-emptying and negation mentioned under the first stage must be accompanied by an empowering and affirmation of the indigenous leaders (Wickeri 2005, 506).

6.4.7 Emphasizing spirituality above all else

Where the emphasis in this working team is spiritual, they will work very well together despite the many cultural differences between them. That is the only way you can explain how Olive Doke and Paul Kasonga worked so well together. It has already been noticed that, "Doke was white but Kasonga was black. Olive was female while Kasonga was male. Doke was a missionary but Kasonga was a local person. Doke grew up in the comforts of the developed world while Kasonga grew up in a rural village. Doke enjoyed very good health but Kasonga was a sickly leper" (p. 14). They emphasized the spiritual nature of their work, rather than seeking to show which gender or which culture was better. The result of this was not only a wonderful working relationship but also an almost seamless handover of leadership in Kafulafuta Mission.

6.4.8 Developing mutual accountability structures

Part of the challenge in this second stage is to allow an indigenous system of accountability to synthesize with the missionaries' system so that the two work together. Often the missionaries want to impose the elaborate system of denominational governance from their sending church upon the new churches on the mission field. They forget that they are in a totally different socio-economic environment. It takes generations to grow up in the church and become educated with college degrees to comprehend this, and so the result is undue delay in the handover process. The missionaries need to help the leaders they have nurtured to see the fundamental principles of governance from the Scriptures and give room to the Holy Spirit to enable them to apply these principles in their own cultural context.

The missionaries must seek to work with the local leaders in a context of comradeship and mutual accountability. They should be willing to be corrected (and even rebuked) by the indigenous leaders if they make a mistake, in precisely the same way that they would correct (and even rebuke) the indigenous leaders if they made a mistake. To begin with, this will be very difficult for them, but the missionaries should foster such an environment by insisting that they are leaders together and that they are not perfect. They too can make mistakes. The indigenous leaders should see the missionaries apologizing where they were wrong.

One of the most difficult issues during this stage is that of accountability with respect to money and the control of it. The failure to handle this correctly fans the flames of paternalism and suspicion. As already stated, "The missionaries hold on to the moneybag and use it as a bit in the mouth of a horse to drive it wither-so-ever they wish. In the same way, the local leaders sense this and resent what is happening" (p. 15). So, there is need at the second and third stage to share this control in a growing way. The leadership together – comprising both the missionary and the indigenous leaders – must discuss both the income and the expenditure. They must share a sense of power of the finances. Again this can only be done where there is mutual respect and admiration.

The key here is transparency! Charles Bennett's statement as he wrestled with this issue of money going from the West to fund missions work on the mission field is pertinent at this point: "The key to success is to have open trust relationships in a partnership between equals" (Moreau et al. 2004, 366). Openness is vital, if trust and mutual respect will mature on the mission field. Miss Doke and other Christian missionaries would have been aware and would have sought to emulate the apostle Paul who sought to show this when handling the financial gifts to the churches in Judea, after the churches in Macedonia and Achaia were already established. He ensured maximum transparency (see 2 Cor 8 and 9).

It is this transparency and atmosphere of mutual accountability that prepares the mission for the handover process. Bill Knipe, a missionary who recently finished this process in Zambia, bore witness to this important principle during an interview for this research.

> I do believe that the best pastor for a Zambian is a Zambian and that every missionary best be aiming at that goal. I have handed over Immanuel Baptist Church to a national pastor. Although I have made my mistakes, I see that the victory lies in keeping an open communication with the man/men I am working with. We discussed very openly everything from finances to ways that my being a missionary might hinder the work. After we handed over the church, the pastor felt at ease to ask me not to return until I was invited. He wanted to see who would remain after I left. He said this would show him who was coming for a Word-centred ministry and who was coming for a man-centred ministry. I made it a habit to follow his counsel, to listen to him and follow him even when I might have thought there was a better way. That created open communication and a sense of equality, as we are both equally dependent on each other as brothers in Christ (Knipe 2010).

6.4.9 Ensuring respect and admiration are mutual

Respect and admiration must not be a one-way street. Both missionaries and indigenous leaders must publicly express their appreciation and admiration for each other. It helps to foster a good working relationship if they can see that their labours and sacrifice are being appreciated. This is what Kasonga ensured was done for Doke on two occasions while he was the leading elder at Kafulafuta, and Doke ensured that when Kasonga died, she wrote his biography. Where do you find missionaries writing biographies of indigenous leaders today? It is very, very rare. But this showed that the two had a great working relationship. They respected and admired each other.

6.5 The third stage of missions

This third stage of the work of missions is about the final handover process so that the missionaries either work under the local leadership or move on to another area to continue the work that they believe God has called them to do. This is the terminus of missions – when it is totally indigenized. In other words, the missionaries must deliberately be working themselves out of a job. They should be looking forward to the day when they become dispensable. This is what the greatest missionary, the Lord Jesus Christ, worked towards when he was here on earth. And that is what the apostles also did as they led the next generation of leaders to take over their work.

6.5.1 Trusting in the work of the Holy Spirit

This is where trust in the Holy Spirit's work in the hearts of God's matured people comes into play. If the missionaries do not really trust that the Holy Spirit, who has given them the convictions that have made them what they are, can also do the same in the hearts of these leaders whom he has nurtured, then they will overstay their welcome. They will want to always be there, playing a supervisory role. Allen confessed, "It is not easy for us today so to trust the Holy Ghost. We can more easily believe in his work in us and through us, than we can believe in his work in and through our converts; we cannot trust our converts to him" (1991, vii).

6.5.2 Taking a secondary role in leadership

One of the greatest challenges at this stage is the need for the missionaries, even when they do not move on to something else but remain in the leadership, to take a secondary role in the church's leadership. This researcher posits that where there is a climate of mutual respect and admiration, this will not be difficult for the missionaries. However, where this handover is simply a fulfilment of a road map or system, or where leadership is merely tokenism, this final handover is very difficult. The missionaries know they cannot really work under the kind of people they are handing over the work to – and they are not even sure that they can carry a quality work forward. Hence, even when they have handed over, they still remain in charge in the shadows.

The researcher interviewed a Baptist pastor, Curtis Chirwa, who had worked with foreign missionaries for about five years. He spoke about this very matter.

> Missionaries should have a deliberate policy towards handing over the leadership of the work to the nationals. Usually, when a missionary starts work and finds a national to work with he should state the work plan to him after training him. I have never heard of any missionary doing this. For instance, missionaries cannot just be working or planting a church without a deadline or a target; that is very discouraging to the national pastor who has been waiting and praying for the handover of the church to him. A policy, say five years, can be good enough for a missionary to hand over a church to a national pastor and then he (the missionary) moves on to start another work. That way they will achieve a lot in the work of missions, rather than staying at one place for over twenty years, probably waiting for their children to grow up who in due course will take over the work (Chirwa 2010).

Another indigenous pastor (Manasseh Kaonga) said in an interview:

Missionaries must deliberately include serious minded nationals who are likely to continue the work after them. Missionaries must realize that they can benefit the nationals up to a certain point, after which the mantle must be passed on completely and they must remain in the background without interference. As hard as that may be, they must trust God by placing confidence in the people whom they have trained (Kaonga 2010).

It was not only the indigenous leaders who were of this opinion but the missionaries too. Nathan Washer (a missionary's son, who later became a missionary too), when interviewed for this research, said:

Once a responsibility in the church is turned over to a national, the missionary must never take it back. The missionary must understand that not everything will be done just the way he/she would do it. There must be room to allow the national man to develop and learn. When the church chooses a new leader and a national man is voted in, the missionary must be able to blend into the background (rare) or he needs to leave (Washer 2010).

Sometimes, it is not just the missionaries who want to remain in charge but the indigenous leaders may also want them to stay. This is because, as Allen rightly observed (1991, 57–58), they know that there are advantages in having the foreign missionaries as their leaders. They can return home and plead for funding, which would help with financial demands on the mission field. They know that once they lose the missionaries, they will also lose these benefits. The missionaries should be wary of this. They should have begun much earlier to show the church that part of their maturing is for them to reach self-government and self-supporting levels. The apparent loss of foreign income is an actual gain.

It is the loss that children in the home suffer when they leave home to set up their own home. They now must work for their food. And yet, that loss is a gain because it shows that they are now a grown-up and are ready to take on the challenges of adulthood. It was the same sense of loss that the disciples did not want to go through when Jesus announced his departure. But it was necessary for them.

The missionaries need to start this educative process very early, even as they are discipling the potential leaders (during the second stage). The principle of incarnational ministry must be inculcated in them so that they are not looking forward to living like the missionaries but like their own people. The missionaries should have tried their best to come down to the economic levels of the people that they are ministering to, but often they will still live above them – especially as they raise their families. However, once the principle has been appreciated and seen in the lives of the missionaries, the context of mutual respect and admiration will yield similar attitudes in the new leaders, which will make them deliberately financially independent of the missionaries' sending churches. It is the leaders who most show this attitude who will gain the highest admiration from the missionaries.

6.5.3 Being set apart for the next phase

The missionaries should allow themselves to be 'set apart' for the new phase of their work by the leadership of the new church that has been planted. This will speak eloquently to the newly established church that they are not above the new leaders, but are seeking to work under them in the new assignment – though still with the support of their sending churches. Thus any new 'ordinations' will be done by this new leadership and not by the missionaries. If they could 'set apart' those who were once their leaders, why can they not ordain everyone else coming after them?

Allen wrote (as quoted earlier on p.51):

> This attitude is apparent everywhere. . . . The moment it is suggested that a council in which natives are in a majority should have the power to direct the action of a white missionary, the moment it is suggested that a native, even though he may be a man of the highest devotion and intellectual ability, should be put into a position of authority in a province where white men still hold office, the white missionaries revolt. They

> will not hear of such a thing. We acknowledge that the Spirit
> of God has fitted the man for a position of authority, but he
> cannot occupy it because we are there (Allen 1991, 143).

This attitude shows that the missionaries have no respect and admiration for the leaders that they have nurtured or have a spirit of pride at the least. The observation in chapter 3 of how Paul and Barnabas placed themselves under the leadership in Antioch, although they were the apostles, is pertinent here. We must follow their example. They could do this because they had worked with these leaders in a context of mutual respect and admiration. They knew the quality of men they were working with and gladly handed over the reins of leadership to them.

This is what caused the breakdown in relationships between the Baptist Mission of Zambia and the Baptist Convention of Zambia (see p. 54). Instead of the Baptist Mission of Zambia handing over the tools of ministry to the Baptist Convention of Zambia, they formed a parallel structure and then held onto the tools of ministry. The two became totally autonomous, yet working together. This frustrated the indigenous leaders to no end until the breach occurred. If the Baptist Mission of Zambia had taken the example of Paul and Barnabas, this would have never happened. As Lumba rightly commented, "There is no scriptural, historical or practical reason for a dual administration in a field where a church of like persuasion and common loyalty exists, especially a church which is the result of the mission's effort" (1995, 32).

Thankfully, that was not the case with Olive Doke. She ensured that Paul Kasonga was part of the leadership of the mission itself in 1931. No dual administration here! It is also evident in the way Olive Doke took a secondary position when Paul Kasonga had become a fully-fledged leader of the church in Kafulafuta. She would listen quietly for many hours when invited to sit in eldership meetings because she knew that she had handed over the work to Kasonga and his fellow elders.

6.6 Conclusion

This is the way in which we can transform paternalism into partnership. There is a real need to emphasize these lessons and steps in order to ensure that church-planting missions ends on a happy note. This researcher has deliberately addressed the area of attitudes rather than that of systems. This is where his one criticism of Lumba's thesis remains (p. 56). Although Lumba saw that the problem was one of wrong attitudes, when he came to formulate the answer he does not come up with a model that corrects the attitudes. Instead he simply wants Africans to take the work of missions seriously. The point this researcher is making is that unless the issue of attitudes is dealt with, the African church will repeat the paternalism of the Western church when their own missionaries are sent out. This is why the model that this researcher is proposing goes to the heart of attitude change.

On the other hand, Mulemfo put his finger on the right way forward when he wrote that African church leaders and expatriate missionaries ". . . need to try and build an environment conducive to reconciliation, repentance, forgiveness, fellowship, service, proclamation, and dialogue. These qualities would play an important role in their common missionary endeavour and would demonstrate their oneness in Jesus Christ" (Mulemfo 2001, 18). This is what the model presented in this chapter seeks to achieve. It is one way to transform paternalism into true partnership.

This researcher is convinced that as difficult as this road map may be, especially because the natural tendency for us all is to hold on permanently to that which we have started, it must still be done. It must be done not simply because it works but because it is what the Bible teaches. Our respect for the Bible is what will make us yield to this approach, even when it is not the most common approach in missions and may seem humiliating on our part.

The researcher would like to reiterate that where an ambience of mutual respect and admiration has been fostered, this handover of the work of missions will be done successfully and happily.

In fact, even where there are differences of opinions on secondary matters, where there is mutual respect and admiration, if there is to be a parting of ways, it will be done in a wholesome way.

CHAPTER 7

Conclusion and Final Recommendations

7.1 The hypothesis proved

This thesis began with a search for an answer to the perennial problem that haunts the work of missions; namely, the trauma that many go through at the terminus of missions when the pioneer missionaries have to hand over the work to indigenous leaders. The researcher put forward a hypothesis, that where mutual respect and mutual admiration are fostered between the missionary and the potential local leaders, the handover process is likely to go smoothly.

By a biblical interpretation of missions (chapter 3) and an analysis of the lives of Olive Doke and Paul Kasonga (chapters 4 and 5), the researcher believes that he has proved this hypothesis. In each of these cases, it was not mere systems that achieved the smooth and seamless handover process that was experienced but rather it was an emphasis on spirituality and a reliance on the work of the Holy Spirit.

Using what was observed in both the interpretation of missions in the Bible and the analysis of the lives of Olive Doke and Paul Kasonga, the researcher proceeded to build a strategy that can help those who are involved in missions to realize such a seamless handover process (chapter 6). Since the burden of the researcher is not merely historical but primarily pastoral and practical, this strategy was very important. It is what the churches need to consider implementing in order to have God-glorifying handover processes in the work of missions in the world. And as Africa picks up the mantle for the work of missions, the researcher prays that these lessons and this strategy will be taken to heart.

The research has reached its destination. The stated aim was to find "how best to engage in the process of pioneering missionaries handing over their work to indigenous leaders so that the process becomes a blessing rather than a curse – as it has often proved to be" (1.1). The researcher's thesis was that "a sensitive handover process is not built on mere systems and agreements but on a foundation of mutual respect and growing admiration between pioneer missionaries and indigenous leaders" (1.1). Through an empirical study, using a case study method as his primary data (1.4), it seems that this hypothesis has been conclusively reached.

7.2 Some pertinent lessons

The chief lesson that has been learned in the preceding chapters is that where there is mutual respect and mutual admiration, there you will find a smooth handover taking place from the church planting missionary to the indigenous leaders. This is precisely what we find in the biblical study and from the study of the lives of Olive Doke and Paul Kasonga. What are some of the pertinent lessons that can be picked from both the biblical survey and the biographical study?

(1) A potential missionary's background or training is foundational in order to secure an attitude of respect and later admiration for the indigenous people.

(2) An appreciation of the culture of the people among whom a missionary is going to serve helps to destroy a paternalistic spirit and fosters respect for them.

(3) Missionaries need to begin working themselves out of a job from the beginning of their ministries. Indigenization is an essential ingredient of missions work.

(4) Some legitimate form of paternalism is inevitable in the first stage of the work, because a missionary comes to give what the indigenous people do not have.

(5) The indigenous people also help to foster a paternalistic spirit in missionaries, hence the need for the missionaries to work extra hard to teach the people a biblical worldview that makes them see the missionaries as their equals.

(6) The attitude of the missionary and indigenous leaders will grow from respect to admiration as they see in each other a right understanding of the Bible and an above-average zeal and giftedness in leadership and teaching.

(7) The attitude of the missionary and indigenous leaders will also grow in respect and admiration towards each other as they see how the other side subjects their culture to the touchstone of Scripture, and obeys whatever the Bible teaches.

(8) The right choice of leaders is critical to the future of the work of missions. Hence, the missionary must not rush and must use biblical criteria in choosing leaders.

(9) Ignorance of one another feeds suspicion, while knowledge of one another feeds mutual respect. Hence, there is need for missionaries and indigenous leaders to know one another as much as possible.

(10) A context of mutual accountability fosters mutual respect between missionary and indigenous leaders, and it shows humility on the part of the missionary.

(11) "The love of money is a root of all kinds of evil". Money issues must be handled in absolute transparency or else they will breed divisions and kill mutual respect.

(12) There is need for the missionaries to trust in the Holy Spirit if they are to hand over the work to indigenous leaders. He who has produced godly desires in them will also produce the same godly desires in the indigenous leaders.

(13) The work of missions is only over when the missionaries have worked themselves out of a job. Hence, the missionaries should be willing to take a secondary role in the work, and even be set apart for any work by the new indigenous leadership.

7.3 Universal application

The fact that the case study was limited to one missionary and one indigenous leader in what was called Lambaland then, and is now largely synonymous to the Copperbelt Province of Zambia, does not mean that the principles can only apply in that region. Similarly, the fact that the case study was among Baptists should not mean that the lessons learned can only be applied by Baptists. The researcher would like to see effort made to apply these principles more widely.

The researcher has taken pains to show this in two ways. First, he has done a biblical interpretation of mission in order to show that the same principles were true as the Lord Jesus Christ was handing over the church to the apostles, and when the apostles were handing over the work to the next generation of leaders. Second, he has done this by weaving into his final analysis the experience and aspirations of other present day missionaries and indigenous leaders. It has become evident, even through these many voices, that the cry for mutual respect and admiration is the same, and that where these two ingredients are present, the handover process has been smooth and successful.

7.4 Suggestions for further research

As the researcher delved into the subject matter for this research, there were other issues arising that time could not allow the researcher to further investigate. Hence, he proposes three areas of further research:

(1) **Females in ministry and missions:** How did the femaleness of Olive Doke impact her work as a leader within the context of her pioneer missionary work?

(2) **Dangers in male/female intimacy:** What dangers did Olive Doke and Paul Kasonga expose themselves to by working so closely together on the mission field?

(3) **Finances in the handover process:** How was the whole area of finances handled during the years Olive Doke and Paul Kasonga worked together? So far, there is silence about this in the material that this researcher read, and yet it is almost always the cause of friction between missionaries and indigenous leaders.

7.5 Biographies of Doke and Kasonga

This research cannot end without a further appeal for popular editions of biographies of Olive Doke and Paul Kasonga. The researcher already stated that there is need to redress the absence of biographies of Zambian Baptist leaders on the Zambian market (1.3.1). Today's Christians need to be made aware of the feats of those who have gone ahead of them. They need to see that their present religious benefits were won at great cost. This can only be done as biographies of former Christian leaders are made available.

The researcher already noted the effect of good Christian biographies in previous generations (1.3.2). Men and women need to read the life of Olive Doke to put aside their many excuses for not serving God in their singleness and in uncivilized and dangerous parts of Africa (such as rural areas). They also ought to read the life of Paul Kasonga and put aside their excuses for not serving God because of their alleged inabilities. May this research inspire such a venture!

7.6 The baton is now in our hands

The researcher ends by once again reiterating that his interest is with the on-going work of missions. The baton is now in our hands. Africa is poised to be the next major player in the work of missions. Western missionaries brought Christianity to this continent. It is now the turn of Christians on this continent, and especially Christians south of the Sahara, to take the gospel to regions beyond. Others paid the price. It is Africa's turn to do the same.

In the *Cape Town Commitment* a similar prayer is made for individuals like Olive Doke to arise within today's church: "We long for God to raise up more men and women of grace who will make long-term commitments to live, love and serve in tough places dominated by other religions, to bring the smell and taste of the grace of Jesus Christ into cultures where it is unwelcome and dangerous to do so. This takes patience and endurance, sometimes for a whole lifetime, sometimes unto death" (Birdsall 2010, 31).

It is the prayer of this researcher that this research will only be fuel for the fire of missions. May the reading of this research show that if African Christians can emphasize the Spirit and true spirituality, then churches will be planted around the continent's rural areas and in the 10/40 Window that will be self-governing, self-propagating, and self-supporting. If African missionaries can only ensure that mutual respect and mutual admiration are fostered and nurtured as they are planting churches wherever God sends them, then the handover process to indigenous leaders there will be seamless. In that way they will not only avoid the mistakes of others but will spread the christian faith in a way that best represents its early pioneers. Amen!

The Working Relationship between Olive Doke and Paul Kasonga

Questionnaire

1. What is your name?
2. When were you born?
3. a) What was your father's name?
   b) What was your mother's name?
4. Where do you live?
5. a) What do know you about Paul Kasonga?
   b) From whom do you know these things?
6. a) What do you know about Olive Doke?
   b) From whom do you know these things?
7. What do know you about them working together in the work of the church and spreading the gospel?
8. Do you know of other people that they used to work with in the ministry?

Interviewer:
Name: .... Sign: ....

Date: ....

Oral Interview Responses

Summary

Generally, the oral interview responses were consistent. There were some historical inaccuracies, but these were few and far between. Also, some stories were larger than life – like that of a man who died but came to life again to just put things right in his marriage, and then he died again! This is why oral tradition must be replaced with written records. Stories tend to grow and take on mystical and extraordinary forms unless they are tied down to reality by being recorded in writing when they occur.

Having said that, the retention level of the people interviewed was remarkable, since almost everything was being said from memory. Paul Kasonga died almost sixty years ago!

All the people interviewed spoke about Olive Doke and Paul Kasonga's relationship as one of mutual respect. Some of the people interviewed lived in the days of Paul Kasonga, though they were quite young and easily impressionable. Hence, their views of Paul and Doke are super-heroic, to say the least. None of them were able to give any negative statements about either Paul or Doke.

Paul's medical condition as a leper really stood out in everyone's mind. However, they all spoke of it as a challenge to us able-bodied individuals. In other words, if a man in his condition could do so much, how much more should those of us who are able-bodied do?

List of people interviewed

Fiwale

1. Rev Lydon Pensulo – Director of Ministries, Northern Baptist Association of Zambia
2. Rev Handson Kasabila – resident of Fiwale Hill Mission
3. Mr Godfrey Mambwe – resident of Fiwale Hill Mission
4. Mr Enock Kabamba – resident of Fiwale Hill Mission
5. Mrs Gertrude Litana – former pupil at Kafulafuta Girls' Boarding School
6. Mrs Eliness Mondwe Muthembo – resident of Fiwale Hill Mission
7. Mr Levi Isaac Bwacha – former Commissioner of Zambia Police Service
8. Mrs Naomi Bwacha – resident of Fiwale Hill Mission
9. Senior Chief Mushili Toili Lwebesha – Paramount Chief of the Lamba people, formerly lived in Kafulafuta Mission
10. Rev Hudson Litana – former secretary at Lambaland Baptist churches' meetings
11. Pastor Jackson Kayambwe – Pastor at Fiwale Hills Baptist Church
12. Mr Patrick Litana – resident of Fiwale Hills Mission
13. Mr Harrison Kalima – resident of Fiwale Hills Mission
14. Mrs Elena Spider Cosamu – former resident of Kafulafuta Mission
15. Ms Emma Mutembo – resident of Pontini Village, Fiwale, and former resident of Kafulafuta Mission
16. Ms Dorris Mutembo – former pupil at Kafulafuta Boarding Girls' School taught by Olive Doke
17. Mr Isaac Lwambululwa – Mukolwe Village, Fiwale
18. Mr Jesse Lwebeshe – wife of Chief Mushili, former resident of Kafulafuta Mission

Masaiti

19. Mr Murray Chaka Milambo – former headmaster, Mahatma Ghandi Secondary School
20. Mr Moffat Ngoma – former employee Ndola Rural Native Authority
21. Mr Aggrey Lupunga – former resident Kafulafuta Mission
22. Mrs Neady Chilima – former resident Kafulafuta Mission
23. Mr Isaac Makonko – resident of Kafulafuta Mission and stayed with Paul Kasonga
24. Mr Peter Landani – resident of Kafulafuta Mission
25. Mrs Mercy Lupunga – former pupil at Kafulafuta Boarding Girls' School

Mpongwe

26. Mr Hudson Mwepu Mutembo – former resident Kafulafuta Mission

Ndola

27. Mrs Patricia Chembo Ngoma – former resident of Kafulafuta Mission

Questionnaire on Missionaries/ Nationals Working Relationships

Introduction

I, Conrad Mbewe, am doing a PhD thesis on "Sensitively Handling the Handover Process in Missions – A Case Study of the Lives of Olive Doke and Paul Kasonga". It is with respect to this thesis that this questionnaire has been prepared. It is meant to help me collect data on some of the difficulties experienced in working relationships between missionaries and nationals, which have led to real challenges in achieving a seamless leadership handover process.

The questionnaire is also meant to point out situations where there may have been 'best practice' so that we may learn positive lessons from such situations and seek to emulate them. Since this is a research on leadership handover, the missionaries and nationals being spoken about here are primarily leaders or potential leaders. Hence, nationals should be understood as indigenous leaders.

Also, this questionnaire is not meant to simply be an opportunity to take a swipe at missionaries who, for the most part, have sacrificed a lot for the cause of the gospel. Rather it is meant to help us to learn from some of their mistakes so that we do not repeat them.

Thank you, in advance, for your willingness to participate in answering these questions.

Personal General Experience

1. How long have you worked with missionaries/nationals and in what capacity or relationship?
2. What has been your overall experience in working with missionaries/nationals (i.e. how can you describe it)?

Personal Opinion on Two Issues

3. Do you think that missionaries should have a deliberate policy towards handing over the leadership of the work to nationals? If so, how should that be done?
4. What do you think causes misunderstandings and strained relationships between missionaries and nationals in this handover process? Have you experienced any of this yourself? If so, give a few examples without naming names.

Paternalism and Inferiority Complex

5. (For nationals only) Many people think that there is a spirit of paternalism in many missionaries. Have you experienced this? If so, give a few examples without naming names.
6. (For nationals only) What do you think causes paternalism in missionaries?
7. (For missionaries only) Many people think that there is an inferiority complex and general suspicion and/or lack of trust in nationals. Have you experienced this? If so, give a few examples without naming names.
8. (For missionaries only) What do you think causes inferiority complex and general suspicion and/or lack of trust in nationals?
9. What is it that you see or would not like to see in a missionary/national that would kill your respect and admiration for him?

10. What is it that you see or would like to see in a missionary/national that would stimulate within you respect and admiration for him?

11. What, in your experience, has been the result of a spirit of paternalism or inferiority complex or lack of trust with respect to:

    (a) The relationship between missionaries and nationals; and

    (b) The whole handover process?

Partnership

12. What do you think should be done in order to foster a good working relationship between missionaries and indigenous pastors to ensure that the handover process is done amicably?

Thank you once again for answering all this!

Bibliography

Abendroth, M. 2008. *Jesus Christ The Prince of Preachers*. Leominster: Day One Publications.

Allen, Jack, Dr. 2008. "The Way of the Disciple in Church Planting." *The Journal for Baptist Theology and Ministry* 5 (1), 53–65.

Allen, Roland. 1991 [1962]. *Missionary Methods: St. Paul's or Ours?* Grand Rapids: Wm. B. Eerdmans.

Anderson, Gerald H, ed. 1999. *Biographical Dictionary of Christian Missions*. Grand Rapids: Wm. B. Eerdmans.

McNeely, Helen et al. 1984. Baptist Mission of Zambia Policy Document.

Beaver, R. Pierce. 2009. "The History of Mission Strategy," in Ralph D. Winter and Steven C. Hawthorne, eds., *Perspectives on the World Christian Movement*. Pasadena, CA: William Carey Library.

Bellin, C. 1973. Diamond Jubilee, 1913–1973. Lamba Baptist Mission.

Bevans, Steve. 2012. *Missions as Prophetic Dialogue*. Paper presented at the RFC Transformation of Religious Life: An Action Oriented Initiative in April and May 2012.

Birdsall, Douglas S., and Brown, Lindsay. 2010. *The Cape Town Commitment*. Peabody, Massachusetts: Hendrickson Publishers.

Bosch, David J. 1991. *Transforming Mission: Paradigm Shifts in Theology of Mission*. Maryknoll: Orbis Books.

Bruce, A. B. 1988. *The Training of the Twelve*. Grand Rapids: Tzgel Publications.

Cantrell, Timothy Wendell. 2004. *Building Mature Churches – A Biblical Basis and an African Case Study in Church Planting and Church Strengthening*. Doctoral Thesis. North West University: South Africa.

Carey, S. Pearce. 1993. *William Carey*. Wakeman Trust: London.

Chimfumpa, Isaac. 2010. Personal interview the researcher conducted with him as part of this research.

Chirwa, Curtis. 2010. Personal interview the researcher conducted with him as part of this research.

Cosamu, Elena Spider. 2010. Personal interview the researcher conducted with her as part of this research.

Cross, Arthur J. 1925. *Twenty Years in Lambaland: A Record of Missionary Work among the Lamba-speaking of Northern Rhodesia and Belgian Congo State: Established 1905*. London: Marshall Brothers.

Clarke, Erskine T. 1975. "Experiment in Paternalism: Presbyterians and Slaves in Charleston, South Carolina." *Journal of Presbyterian History* 53, Fall 1975, 223–238.

Cursons, W. E. 1929. *Joseph Doke: The Missionary-Hearted*. Johannesburg: The Christian Literature Depot.

Doke, Clement M. 1931. *The Lambas of Northern Rhodesia*. London: George G Harrap & Company Ltd.

———. 1975. *Trekking in South Central Africa 1913–1919*. Johannesburg: South African Baptist Historical Society.

Doke, O. C. 1931a. "Picking up the threads." Lambaland Newsletter No. 58.

———. 1931b. "The Happenings of a week." Lambaland Newsletter No 59.

———. 1931c. "The Village Baptism." Lambaland Newsletter No 59.

———. 1932a. "African villages move nearer." Lambaland Newsletter No 61.

———. 1932b. "Great Gathering of Native Chiefs." Lambaland Newsletter No 63.

———. 1932c. "Report of the Women's Work" Lambaland Newsletter No 63.

———. 1932d. "Joy in the presence of the angels" Lambaland Newsletter No 63.

———. 1932e. "The Lord goes before" Lambaland Newsletter No 63.

———. 1932f. "Letter from Miss Doke" Lambaland Newsletter No 64.

———. 1933a. "Contemplation" Lambaland Newsletter No. 66.

———. 1933b. "Letter from Miss Doke" Lambaland Newsletter No. 68.

———. 1934a. "Chalwe" Lambaland Newsletter No. 70.

———. 1934b. "Report of the Women's work" Lambaland Newsletter No. 71.

———. 1934c. "A Long trek" Lambaland Newsletter No. 72.

———. 1935. "Jimu" Lambaland Newsletter No. 73.

———. 1937. "Report for the year 1936" Lambaland Newsletter No. 82.

———. 1938a. "Report for year 1937" Lambaland Newsletter No. 86.

———. 1938b. "A Cycle Trek" Lambaland Newsletter No. 88.

———. 1939a. "Chalwe" Lambaland Newsletter No. 89.

———. 1939. "Jonathan" Lambaland Newsletter No. 90.

———. 1939c. "Half-a-Day on a Mission Station" Lambaland Newsletter No. 91.

————. 1940. "Report for Six months ending December 31ˢᵗ [1939]" Lambaland Newsletter No. 94.

————. 1941. "Report from Kafulafuta for Six months ending December 31ˢᵗ, 1940" Lambaland Newsletter No. 97.

————. 1941. "Kafulafuta Area Annual Report" Lambaland Newsletter No. 98.

————. 1942a. "The Awakening of the Lambas" Lambaland Newsletter No. 99.

————. 1942b. "Half yearly report July to December 1941 Kafulafuta Area" Lambaland Newsletter No. 100.

————. 1942c. "Annual Report Kafulafuta Area" Lambaland Newsletter No. 101.

————. 1943. "Letter from Miss Doke" Lambaland Newsletter No. 103.

————. 1944a. "Annual Report Kafulafuta Area 1 July, 1943 – 30 June, 1944" Lambaland Newsletter No. 105.

————. 1944b. "Lambaland Awakening" Lambaland Newsletter No. 105.

————. 1945a. "Tribute to W. A. Phillips" Lambaland Newsletter No. 106

————. 1945b. "Report for Kafulafuta Area for July to December 1944" Lambaland Newsletter No. 107.

————. 1945c. "Heralds of Salvation" Lambaland Newsletter No. 108.

————. 1946a. "Kafulafuta Report July, 1944, to June, 1945." Lambaland Newsletter No. 109.

————. 1946b. "Annual Report-Kafulafuta Area year ending June 30ᵗʰ 1946" Lambaland Newsletter No. 110.

————. 1947. "Answer to Prayer - Love Triumphant" Lambaland Newsletter No. 112.

————. 1951. "Report for the Kafulafuta Area Year ending June, 1951" Lambaland Newsletter No.128.

————. 1953a. "The Ordinations of Three Native Pastors" Lambaland Newsletter No. 136.

————. 1953b. "The Coronation Celebrations in Lambaland" Lambaland Newsletter No. 136.

————. 1954a. "Notes and News" Lambaland Newsletter No. 137.

————. 1954b. "Pen pictures of Native Workers – Paul Kasonga – The Apostle to the Lambas" Lambaland Newsletter No. 139.

Doke Olive C. 1944. Report of the Investigation of Initiation Ceremonies of Northern Rhodesia.

Doke, Olive C. 1955. *Paul the Leper – Apostle to the Lambas.* Johannesburg: South Africa Baptist Missionary Society.

Doke, Olive C. 1963. "Boreham and the Doke Connection." *New Zealand Baptist*, January 1963, 4.

Doke, Olive C. 1964. Unpublished Autobiography.

Doke, Olive C. 1966. "Fifty Years in Lambaland". In *South African Baptist Magazine*, (September), 6–8.

Edmonds, W. T. 1972. In: *South African Baptist Magazine*.

England, Frank and Torquil Paterson, eds. 1989. *Bounty in Bondage: The Anglican Church in Southern Africa*. Johannesburg: Raven Press.

Ephson, I. S. 1969. *Galleries of Gold Coast Celebrities*. Accra: Ilen Publications.

Erlank, Natasha. 2003. "Indigenous Christianity in British Kaffraria after 1850." *Missionalia* 31 (1), 19–41.

Frey, R. L. 2009. History of the Zambia Baptist Association 1905–2005. Limbe, Malawi: Assemblies of God Press.

Gandhi, Mahatma K. 1909. The C. M. Doke Collection of Personal Letters from M. K. Gandhi. UNISA Archives (http://uir.unisa.ac.za/handle/10500/4668). Acc 385.

Greening, Sister. 1934. "Kafulafuta" Lambaland Newsletter No. 69.

Harries, J. 2008. "'Material provision' or preaching the gospel: reconsidering 'holistic' (integral) mission." *Evangelical Review of Theology* 32 (3), 257–270.

Hendriks, H. J. 2004. *Studying congregations in Africa*. Wellington: Lux-Verbi-BM.

Hester, H. I. 1981 (1950), *The Heart of the New Testament*. Nashville: Broadman Press.

Hiebert, Paul G. 1994. *Anthropological Reflections on Missiological Issues*. Grand Rapids: Baker Book House.

Hildebrandt, Jonathan. 1990. *History of the Church in Africa*. Africa Christian Press: Achimoto.

Hudson-Reed Sydney, ed. 1983. *By Taking Heed – The History of Baptists in Southern Africa 1820–1977*. Roodepoort, South Africa: Baptist Publishing House.

———. 1998. *Clement Martyn Doke: Man of two Missions*. Cape Town South African Baptist Historical Society.

Jennings, James R. 1991. "From paternalism to empowerment" in Michael Downey, ed. *That They Might Live: Power, Empowerment, and Leadership in the Church*. New York: Crossroad, 118–129.

Jennings, Peggy. 1965. Little Miss Doke – Missionary Indomitable. In *Horizon*, (July), 13–15, 38.

Jordan, S. 2006. "Paternalism and Roman Catholicism: the English Catholic elite in the long eighteenth century," in *Elite and Popular Religion*. Woodbridge, England: Boydell Press, 272–281.

Kabamba, Enock. 2010. Personal interview conducted by researcher with him as part of this research.

Kaonga, Manasseh. 2010. Personal interview the researcher conducted with him as part of this research.

Keddie, Gordon J. 1993. *You are my Witnesses.* Evangelical Press, Durham.

Kemp, Roger Francis. 1987. *South African Baptist Missionary Society in Zambia: A Missiological Evaluation.* Dissertation, University of South Africa, Pretoria, South Africa.

Knight-Bruce. 1989. "Memories of Mashonaland." *Missionalia.* The Southern African Missiological Society, 171.

Knipe, Bill. 2010. Personal interview the researcher conducted with him as part of this research.

Kostenberger, Andreas J. 2004. *John.* Grand Rapids: Baker Academic.

Kretzschmar, Louise. 1996. *Olive Carey Doke: A Neglected Baptist Pioneer,* in C. Landman, ed. *Digging up Foremothers: Stories of Women in Africa,* Pretoria: UNISA Press, 141–166.

Landani, Peter. 2010. Personal interview the researcher conducted with him as part of this research.

Lefevere, P. 1985. "Moving beyond paternalism." *One World,* (110), 16–17.

Litana, Hudson. 2010. Personal interview the researcher conducted with him as part of this research.

Litana, Patrick. 2010. Personal interview the researcher conducted with him as part of this research.

Little Christopher R. 2005. *Mission In The Way Of Paul, Biblical Mission For The Church In The Twenty-First Century.* Peter Lang Publishing, 61.

Lumba, Thomas Kasongo. 1995. *A Quest for Authentic Practice of Missions in Africa.* Thesis, Baptist theological Seminary, Ruschlikon, Switzerland.

Lwambululwa, Isaac. 2010. Personal interview the researcher conducted with him as part of this research.

Lwebesha, Senior Chief Mushili Toili. 2010. Personal interview the researcher conducted with him as part of this research.

Mandryk, J. 2010. *Operation World – The Definitive Prayer Guide to Every Nation.* Biblica Publishing, Colorado.

Masters, H. and Masters, W. E. 1920. *In Wild Rhodesia: A Story of Missionary enterprise and Adventure in the Land where Livingstone Lived, Laboured and Died.* London: Francis Griffiths.

Mafuka, K. Nyamayaro. 1977. "American Presbyterian Missionaries in South-West Kasai (Congo) 1905–1962." *Journal of the Canadian Church Historical Society* 19 (3–4), 190–207.

Mbewe, Conrad. 2007. *The Importance of Recorded History of the Baptist Church in Zambia for Pastors and the Members of the Church.* MA Thesis, University of Pretoria, South Africa.

Meier, Ira David. 1975. *The Dokes' Contribution to Lambaland.* (Diploma). Baptist Theological College of Southern Africa.

Meiring, Piet G. J. 1980. "Africa as a Receiving and Sending Continent." *Missionalia* 8 (1), 16–24.

Moreau, A. Scott, ed. 2000. *Evangelical Dictionary of World Missions.* Grand Rapids: Baker Book House.

Moreau, A. Scott, Corwin C. Gary, and McGee B. Gary. 2004. *Introducing World Missions: A Biblical, Historical and Practical Survey.* Grand Rapids: Baker Book House.

Mouton, Johann. 2001. *How to Succeed in your Masters and Doctoral Studies.* Pretoria: Van Schaik Publishers.

Mufuka, K. Nyamayaro. 1977. *Missions and Politics in Malawi.* Ontario: Limestone Press.

Mulemfo, M. M. 2001. "Swedish missionary presence in Africa." *Missionalia* 29 (1), 3–20.

Munkumba, Michael. 2008. *Relations between Mining MNEs and the local Communities in Zambia and South Africa – creating linkages into the local economy.* PhD Thesis, Erasmus University, Rotterdam.

Mutembo, Hudson Mwepe. 2010. Personal interview the researcher conducted with him as part of this research.

Nettles, T. J. 2009. "James Petigru Boyce: for Christ and his church." *The Southern Baptist Journal of Theology* 13 (1), Spring 2009, 6–28.

Obed, Uzodinma. 2001. *Mobilising Churches in Africa for Missions.* Glory Tabernacle Ministry, Ibadan.

Pearce, Winifred M. 1948. Article on Olive Doke in *The Christian,* August 12.

Pensulo, Lydon. 2010. Personal interview the researcher conducted with him as part of this research.

Pentecost, J. D. 1981, *The Words and Works of Jesus Christ.* Grand Rapids: Zondervan.

Phiri, Lazarus. 2005. *Brethren in Christ Mission in Zambia, 1906–1978: A Historical Study of Western Missionary Leadership Patterns and the Emergence of Tonga Church Leaders.* PhD Thesis, University of Edinburgh.

Piper John. 1993. *Let the Nations be Glad: The Supremacy of God in Missions.* Grand Rapids: Baker Books.

Presler, Titus. 1989. Missionary Anglicanism Meets an African Religion." *Missionalia* 17 (3), 162–175.

Rooy, S. H. 2006. *The Theology of Missions in the Puritan Tradition: A Study of Representative Puritans.* Audobon Press: Laurel, MS, USA.

Russel, H. O. 1983. *The Baptist Witness – A Concise Baptist History.* El Paso, Texas: Carib Baptist Publications.

Saayman Willem. 2001. "Racism and mission enthusiasm." *Missionalia* 29 (3), 476–485.

Saunders, Davis Lee. 1973. *A History of Baptists in East and Central Africa.* Dissertation, Southern Baptist Theological Seminary.

Siegel, Brian. 1999. *The Kafulafuta Mission in Zambia* [online]. Furman University, Greenville. Available from http://www.ecu.edu/africa/sersas/BrianSiegel.htm. [Accessed 5 September 2007].

Smylie, J. H. 1981. "The Bible, race and the changing South." *Journal of Presbyterian History* 59, 197–217.

Sparrow, Olive. 1972. In *South African Baptist Magazine,* (May).

Spencer, Leon P. 1982. "Christianity and colonial protest: Perceptions of W. E. Owen, Archbishop of Kavirondo." *Journal of Religion in Africa* 13 (1), 46–60.

Stott, John R. W. 1990. *The Message of Acts.* Leicester: InterVarsity Press.

Strauch, Alexander. 1995. *Biblical Eldership – An Urgent Call to Restore Biblical Church Leadership.* Littleton: Lewis and Roth Publishers.

Times of Zambia, 28 September 1966, editorial.

Thornbury, John. 1996. *David Brainerd – Pioneer Missionary to the American Indians.* Darlington: Evangelical Press.

Vaughan, Curtis. 1974. *Bible Study Commentary: Acts.* Grand Rapids: Zondervan.

Washer, Nathan. 2010. Personal interview the researcher conducted with him as part of this research.

Wickeri, P. L. 2005. "Roland Allen and the Decolonisation of Christianity." *Missionalia* 33 (3).

Wiersbe, Warren W. 1987. *Be Diligent: A Commentary on Mark.* Wheaton: Scripture Press Publications.

Williams, K. F. 1995. "Providence, Paternalism, Prejudice and Policy: A consideration of Wesleyan missionary, Frederick Mason's critique of Native Policy in Natal in 1906." *Studia Historiae Ecclesiasticae* 21 (2), 44–56.

Winter, Ralph D. and Hawthorne, Steven C, ed. 2009. *Perspectives on the World Christian Movement – A Reader.* Carlisle: Paternoster Press.

Wright, Christopher J. H. 2006. *The Mission of God.* Nottingham: InterVarsity Press.

Wright, E. E. 2010. *A Practical Theology of Missions – Dispelling the Mystery; Recovering the Passion.* Leominster: Day One Publications.

Langham Literature and its imprints are a ministry of Langham Partnership.

Langham Partnership is a global fellowship working in pursuit of the vision God entrusted to its founder John Stott –

to facilitate the growth of the church in maturity and Christ-likeness through raising the standards of biblical preaching and teaching.

Our vision is to see churches in the majority world equipped for mission and growing to maturity in Christ through the ministry of pastors and leaders who believe, teach and live by the Word of God.

Our mission is to strengthen the ministry of the Word of God through:

- nurturing national movements for biblical preaching
- fostering the creation and distribution of evangelical literature
- enhancing evangelical theological education

especially in countries where churches are under-resourced.

Our ministry

Langham Preaching partners with national leaders to nurture indigenous biblical preaching movements for pastors and lay preachers all around the world. With the support of a team of trainers from many countries, a multi-level programme of seminars provides practical training, and is followed by a programme for training local facilitators. Local preachers' groups and national and regional networks ensure continuity and ongoing development, seeking to build vigorous movements committed to Bible exposition.

Langham Literature provides majority world pastors, scholars and seminary libraries with evangelical books and electronic resources through grants, discounts and distribution. The programme also fosters the creation of indigenous evangelical books for pastors in many languages, through training workshops for writers and editors, sponsored writing, translation, strengthening local evangelical publishing houses, and investment in major regional literature projects, such as one volume Bible commentaries like *The Africa Bible Commentary*.

Langham Scholars provides financial support for evangelical doctoral students from the majority world so that, when they return home, they may train pastors and other Christian leaders with sound, biblical and theological teaching. This programme equips those who equip others. Langham Scholars also works in partnership with majority world seminaries in strengthening evangelical theological education. A growing number of Langham Scholars study in high quality doctoral programmes in the majority world itself. As well as teaching the next generation of pastors, graduated Langham Scholars exercise significant influence through their writing and leadership.

To learn more about Langham Partnership and the work we do visit **langham.org**